IRISH FARMING LIFE

Irish Farming Life

History and Heritage

JONATHAN BELL

&

MERVYN WATSON

FOUR COURTS PRESS

Typeset in 11 pt on 14 pt Garamond by
Carrigboy Typesetting Services for
FOUR COURTS PRESS LTD
7 Malpas Street, Dublin 8, Ireland
www.fourcourtspress.ie
and in North America for
FOUR COURTS PRESS
c/o ISBS, 920 NE 58th Avenue, Suite 300, Portland, OR 97213.

A catalogue record for this title is available
from the British Library.

ISBN 978–1–84682–531–6 pbk

Printed in Spain
by Castuera, SA.

Contents

Preface

> The history of Ireland was such a tale of misery and wretchedness, enough to make the angels howl and stamp their golden feet.[1]

KARL MARX SAW THE HISTORY of the world as the history of different forms of oppression, a view that is easy to accept when we look at Irish history for most of the last millennium. Europeans began to refer to 'poor' Ireland in the late seventeenth century, and during the next 250 years most travellers and other observers spent a lot of time pondering how things had gone so badly wrong there. In the 1950s, it was claimed that borstal boys in England immediately knew that the phrase 'That sad and beautiful country' could only refer to Ireland.[2] If this was the whole story, Irish history would indeed be a nightmare from which we should try to awaken. Fortunately, as Marx also recognized, the history of the world is also the history of how people overcome obstacles, to find freedom and well-being against all the odds. The history of Irish farming is one such story of achievement. During the last 300 years, Irish farmers have developed and adopted implements and techniques that have made agriculture a mainstay of the economy, north and south. Culturally and socially, Irish farming society has displayed high levels of decency and creativity, developing systems of mutual support and an expressive culture of music and poetry still celebrated by many Irish people, despite the onslaught of globalisation.

This book deals with both the history and heritage of farming in Ireland. By history, we mean the past as described and interpreted by scholars. We use the term heritage, on the other hand, to describe how the past is presented in art, folklore, drama, music, poetry, literature, films, re-enactments and museum displays. History and heritage often overlap, but can also be opposing ways of looking at the past. History, at its best, questions existing assumptions and interpretations. Heritage, on the other hand, often revels in entrenched stereotypes in ways that can be very amusing, or very dangerous. Heritage products range from high art to embarrassing vulgarities.

In the quest for historical truth, the connection between heritage and history can be very positive. The creativity of heritage work often enriches and enlivens historical analysis, and can sometimes help historians transcend their own prejudices. An unhealthy overlap between historical analysis and heritage creations can also be very clear though, when we look at the kinds of explanations that appear in some bad historical research. Historical discussion should be open-minded and sceptical, with researchers prepared to reject even dearly held views if the evidence requires it. However, as in heritage productions, stereotypes and associated prejudices can appear in historical accounts in very thin disguise, in what purport to be high-level academic studies. This can be particularly obvious when historians discuss specific topics in the light of the approach broadly described as revisionism. We first became aware of revisionism, and some of our own prejudices, in the 1970s, when discussing evictions and the fear of eviction in nineteenth-century Ireland. Our position was based on the view that evictions were a very bad thing. We were amazed when a well-respected historian told us that some scholars believed that there hadn't been enough evictions. He went on to explain that, according to this revisionist view, the Irish economy would have been much more efficient if more people had been cleared off the land. We took the view that a good economy was one that ensured the well-being of people participating in it, something that evictions clearly did not do. We decided that not only evictions were bad, so was revisionism.

It seemed that some revisionists also saw Irish landlords as struggling to develop their estates in the face of their tenants' laziness, or more politely, 'high leisure preference'. We were new to the study of farming history, but we knew enough to appreciate the desperate ingenuity and back-breaking work involved in securing survival on small farms, so this was another black mark against revisionism. However, we had to think again when a scholar whose work we respected very much, Bruce Campbell, pointed out that our own approach was 'revisionist', in that it attempted to overturn an established stereotype of Irish farmers as irrationally prejudiced against improvement, by showing the abundant evidence for creativity and risk-taking in changing farming methods. We had to agree with this, and admit that revisionism wasn't all wrong!

There is no final solution to the problem of distortions that can arise in either historical or heritage work because of our own, inevitably partial viewpoints, but one way to minimise the extent of this distortion is to let the people whose lives are being studied speak for themselves, an approach that is central to a lot of heritage work. Much of the material presented in this book is based on data collected during fieldwork by folklorists, oral historians and social anthropologists. One of the strengths of these subjects is that they also try to base their analysis on people's own understanding of their experience. Historians who see quantification as the most authoritative and objective approach to analysis, sometimes disparage the use of people's testimonies as anecdotal, but this view misses something important. Quantification, where it is possible, is of central importance in developing an authoritative historical overview, but at best it shows patterns resulting from past behaviour, not the goals and wishes that directed it. The accounts of people who made the histories we study give (problematic) access to the motivation and strategies that have directed action, aspects of experience that quantitative analysis can only approach through speculation. In the study of Irish farming history, individual testimonies can be used to build a credible model of Irish rural life, which, while recognising human stupidity and wickedness, presents the history of Irish agriculture as a story of achievement, based on evidence that is part of both history and heritage.

The extent to which we depend on other people's research in this book will be obvious, particularly the work of anthropologists such as Anthony Cohen, Rosemary Harris and Hugh Brody, folklorists like Anne O'Dowd, and historians such as David Fitzpatrick, Heather Holmes and Joanna Bourke. We have also included quotations from poetry, novels and songs, hopefully to give pleasure as well as providing insights. Philip Flanagan's series of paintings are included to show how awareness of visual aspects of heritage can be abstracted in the same way as a piece of music, but still evoke the changing beauty of the Irish landscape, a backdrop to the lives described, and a centrally important element in what we intend to be a celebration of Irish rural life.

The book is based on more than thirty years of work in the Ulster Folk and Transport Museum. A lot of cerebral dust can gather in that time, and we apologise if this is visible. The subject itself is always fresh and exciting, and we hope that this shines through the dust.

A lot of people contributed to the production of the book. In our years of fieldwork we relied on a number of mentors who shared their expertise with us with patience and courtesy. These include Malachy McSparran, Joe Kane, Bertie Hanna, Dolly McRoberts, John and Elsie Andrews, Fred Coll, Hugh Paddy Óg Ward and Dan Laverty. Friends and colleagues from other institutions who gave help and support include Martin Fanning, Michael Maloney, Toddy Doyle, Patricia O'Hare, Séamas MacPhilib, Clodagh Doyle, Robbie Hannan, Robert Berry, Liam Corry, Lesley Simpson and Madeleine McAllister. Patricia Stratford gave us advice and encouragement as always, and Patrick Stratford shared his photographic skills with patience and generosity. We are also grateful for institutional help from the National Museum of Ireland, the Ulster Folk and Transport Museum, the National Library of Ireland, Muckross Traditional Farms and Library, Down County Museum and the Agriculture Library of Queen's University Belfast.

Acknowledgments

THE QUOTATIONS FROM the work of Patrick Kavanagh are reprinted from *Collected Poems*, edited by Antoinette Quinn (Allen Lane, 2004) and from *Tarry Flynn* (Penguin Books, 1978) by kind permission of the Trustees of the Estate of the late Katherine B. Kavanagh, through the Jonathan Williams Literary Agency.

The lines from John Hewitt's 'Glenaan' and from 'Country Speech' are reprinted by kind permission of Dr Keith Millar.

Quotations from John McGahern's novel *The Dark* (1965) are reprinted by kind courtesy of the estate of John McGahern and by permission of Faber and Faber.

Chapter 1

Country people talking

THIS BOOK IS ABOUT THE PAST, but also about the way people remember the past, and how and why they celebrate it. We hope to highlight both the complexity of Irish farming history during the last 250 years, and the shared elements that unified it. Ireland is a small country, but the contrasts within it can be startling. In farming, these contrasts are clear when we look at data related to, for example, farm size (Figs. 1 and 2). In the 1770s, the great agricultural improver, Arthur Young, visited a Mr McCarthy whose farm in Tipperary, he concluded, must be 'the most considerable one in the world'. This tenant farmer had 10,000 sheep, more than 1,100 cattle (including 80 plough bullocks), and 180 horses.[1] At the same time, by contrast, millions of desperately poor people were surviving on holdings where the ownership of one cow made survival at a subsistence level possible. Faced with contrasts of this kind, it is obvious that almost any general statement about rural society in the past can only be made with caution, emphasising the extent to which human beings escape any rigid categorisation. However, there were important aspects of life that were common throughout the country and we hope to identify these. The main subject of the book is the working life of Irish farming people, and some of the ways this shaped their personal and social relationships. Working arrangements imposed a lot of constraints on other aspects of people's lives and these produced identifiable social structures – as well as the anomalies and contradictions created by individuals and groups who found ways to bend or break the rules, creating the diversity that makes the subject as interesting as it is challenging.

The complexity of Irish rural society was partly the result of huge global changes that have occurred in the last 300 years, which had different impacts at local levels. However, in the long term, some changes came to all parts of the country, and some major events brought similar changes everywhere within a very short time. For example, what was happening in almost any area in the decades before the Great Famine of the 1840s was very different indeed from what was happening in the same area around 1900, when there were smaller acreages of crops and fewer people almost everywhere.

1 Haymaking on the Clonbrock demesne farm, Ahascragh, County Galway, *c*.1900. By the late nineteenth century, implements used on large farms were manufactured as part of a global trade. (Photo: Clonbrock coll., National Library of Ireland.)

The time scale covered in our study changes with the subject discussed, but in general we are trying to include people's own models of their past, so we are concentrating on the last hundred years when the value of recording ordinary lives became more widely appreciated. During this recent past, oral testimonies began to be recorded in detail, and local studies have proliferated. We rely a lot on both of these sources, as well as the illustrative material that became very detailed with the introduction of photography. We also use Irish literature of the last 200 years as a source; these works have reinforced or modified popular models of the past, deepened (and sometimes distorted) historical understanding, and continue to give pleasure.

Oral history

Oral history became popular with local history societies and community groups in the 1970s, when cassette tape recorders became common. After a

2 Farm near Crolly, County Donegal, *c.*1900. Many families in the west of Ireland survived on less than five acres of arable land. The potato made this possible, if sufficient manure was available from a cow, supplemented near the coast by seaweed. Oats were the only other significant crop, oat straw being used as fodder instead of hay. (Photo: Lawrence coll. R1380, National Library of Ireland.)

3 Connemara people in 1892. (Photo: Tuke coll., National Library of Ireland.)

4 Siobhán McKenna as Pegeen in the film version of Synge's *Playboy of the Western World.* (Gael-Linn record cover.)

few years, however, the excitement lessened, and people are now generally less confident that switching on a recorder will open a gateway to the past. The reasons for this caution have been widely discussed. The following brief outline of some of the issues raised is based on our own experience of recording people during fieldwork, and also of using accounts based on oral testimonies.

Irish country people, like people anywhere, express themselves in very different ways. To a large extent, the diversity of these styles of communication reflect regional differences as well as differences in social class, so they act as a metaphor for the complexity of other aspects of rural life, including farming. The situation becomes even more complicated when we look at conversations recorded in literature, where the style of communication is shaped not only by the social and regional background of the person recorded, but also by the creativity of the author. Written accounts of rural Ireland sometimes record a style of speech that seems full of highly wrought eloquence, but there are good reasons for treating these with caution. John Millington Synge, for example, attempted to capture the poetic style of Irish speakers in his great plays set in the west of Ireland and the Aran Islands (Fig. 4). In Act 1, scene 1, of *The Playboy of the Western World*, Shawn tells Pegeen that on his way to visit her,

> I stood for a while outside … and I could hear the cows breathing, and sighing in the stillness of the air, and not a step moving any place from this gate to the bridge.[2]

This is very beautiful image, but it is difficult to imagine anyone in modern rural Ireland talking in such a way without provoking derision. It has been claimed that Aran Islanders who remembered Synge were not always impressed either, finding his melancholy manner and doom-laden declamations somewhat ridiculous. When his name was mentioned, some of them would laugh and say, 'Ochone, ochone!' (Alas, alas!).[3] On the other hand, however, when it seems appropriate, Irish people are quite capable of putting on a performance which includes wildly overwrought avowals. Quentin Crisp, describing his outrageous gay life in early twentieth-century London, for example, was charmed by some of the young Irish men he encountered on his adventures, and their approach to the elderly gay men they did business with.

> If Italian is the language of song, Irish is the voice of flattery. From the lips of these young men I have heard phrases so archaic and hyperboles so florid that even Mr Synge could not have used them without a giggle.[4]

The willingness of many Irish people to talk and talk can be seen as an admirable cultural trait, or a national weakness. As young fieldworkers in the early 1980s, we dreaded interviewing people noted for 'country craic'. On one trip to County Tyrone, we spent four hours talking to one clever and friendly man. We intended to find out about local techniques of saving turf, but came away having recorded this for about ten minutes. The rest of the time he told us jokes and stories and explained his ideas for exploiting Ireland's peat bogs. (Their soft surface would make them ideal landing sites for 'paraquootists' and their fibrous top layers could be compressed into a type of felt, ideal for making suits and hats.) A lot of our early impatience with this conversational style disappeared with the years, and the realisation that in a world with no radio or television, and dim lighting, the ability to stretch out a story or a song would have been highly valued. However, we still preferred interviewing people who got to the point in question without elaboration.

People like this were not hard to find. Many country people, especially in the north of the country, delight in stoical and inexpressive statements, and often lapse into silence in a way that city dwellers might find slightly uncomfortable.[5] John Hewitt celebrated this terseness in a poem about people in the Glens of Antrim.

> Often the wisest have no more style than a sod …
> You will remember that woman whose house we passed …
> A squad of children calling and running about;
> And you said, 'You have a lovely wee family here,'
> And she, 'Och well, they have all their features, thank God.'[6]

Samuel Beckett's brilliantly ponderous account of the detail in which many country people note even the smallest event also evokes a distinctive mode of communication.

> It would appear on reflection that Sapo's departure can seldom have escaped [the Lamberts] … For at the very least movement within sight of their land, were it only that of a little bird alighting or taking to wing, they raised their heads and stared with wide eyes. And even on the road, of which segments were visible more than a mile away, nothing could happen without their knowledge, and they were able to identify all those who passed along it and whose remoteness reduced them to the size of a pin's head, but also to divine whence they were coming, where they were going, and for what purpose. Then they cried the news to one another, for they often worked at a great distance apart, or they exchanged signals, all erect and turned towards the event, for it was one, before bowing themselves to the earth again.[7]

This attention to detail can strike city dwellers as odd. A Belfast woman we were told about was taken aback when her neighbour in her new home in County Fermanagh commented on her washing line, 'I see you washed your red towel last week'. Scrutiny of this intensity can be unnerving at a personal level, but it also indicates a potentially rich source of historical detail.

Many of our ideas about oral history are based on Gaynor Kavanagh's survey of the subject.[8] We were goaded into thinking about oral history as a research method when a colleague in the Ulster Folk and Transport Museum dismissed the subject as 'collecting wee stories'. This attitude was clearly wrong, based on a failure to recognise the fundamental importance of memory, not only for routine activities like finding our way to work, or cooking a meal, but as a cornerstone of our personality, our sense of who we are. However, our cynical colleague did have a point. Memories can be triggered by cues such as an old song, an old photograph or a smell, and people often find it easier to remember in situations where they feel safe, but these triggers can also lead to the suppression or distortion of what is remembered. Eric Hobsbawm saw this as a fundamental problem:

> Most oral history today is personal memory, which is a remarkably slippery medium for preserving facts … memory is not so much a recording as a selective mechanism, and the selection is, within limits, constantly changing.[9]

If we are using oral evidence to find out what really happened in the past, it is important to understand how distortions can arise, and why. Research into how memories can be restructured has produced some dramatic instances of unconscious change. One well-known example was recorded in England. A woman interviewed about her memories of the day that Britain declared war on Hitler recounted that, 'We were all together in our little living room … [the family] all together for once', when Neville Chamberlain made his historic radio broadcast. She remembered that they were all 'shaken to the roots' by the first siren alert. However, an account that she had written at the time, which came to light later, made it clear that she had not heard either the broadcast or the siren, but was playing the piano, when first her mother came in shouting at her, followed by her father issuing orders and giving useless advice![10] This seems to be an instance of unintended adjustment of memories so that they conform to a normative view – how it should have been. Newsreels of the period often showed a family listening earnestly to the crucial broadcast, a more fitting response than the chaotic reality.

People will often restructure an account to give it a narrative form – make it a better story. They will also tend to recount incidents that reinforce their own views, or prejudices. It will be clear that many of the models of the past used by country people in this book are based on stereotypes of the Irish, the English, landlords, small farmers, the family, and the neighbours. Some elements of these stereotypes can be supported with real evidence, but others are clearly ludicrous. However, they are all relevant to our subject, which is about the past, and also how people use the past to situate themselves in the present.

People do not often organise their memories as part of an academic discipline. In oral history we often deal with people's 'episodic memories'; long-term recollections called up when we remember events, places and people associated with particular periods in our lives. Unless we call up these memories regularly, we do not remember them in a fixed sequence, but as separate episodes linked to major events. These events might be public, such as 'the War' or 'the Troubles', or important events in our personal lives, such as when we started work, or got married. Part of the complex task of using material like this as historical evidence is to produce a map of a person's individual experience that can be matched to more general models of the past.

Despite all the difficulties just outlined, the potential of oral history far outweighs the difficulties. While, as Hobsbawm claimed, memory may be a particularly 'slippery' form of data storage, many of the problems associated with this are also shared with written testimonies; restructuring and selection is at least as likely to occur in the reflective task of writing as in a relaxed interview. Despite the filtering and distortions of memory, the huge advantage oral testimonies have over written accounts is the overwhelming richness of the former as a historical source. Written historical accounts usually require a lot of imaginative reconstruction on the part of scholars attempting to identify the aims and motives of the people whose activities are described. This applies most obviously to statistical records, which record the outcome of activities but not the strategies that underlay them, or the ironies and contradictions arising from the unintended consequences of action. Collecting oral histories allows us to explore people's memories of the goals and feelings that led them to take particular actions. Most obviously, oral testimonies give us access to huge areas of history that have never been previously recorded, and are not accessible in any other way. In oral history, the level of detail available is limited only by the power of recall of the person interviewed, and the time and energy of the collector.

Assessing the evidence

In attempting to assess the accuracy of data collected in oral interviews, we should look for independent corroboration of evidence. Comparison of oral evidence with contemporary documentation, if any is available, is one of the best ways in which we can test factual evidence (for example, acreage of crops, livestock numbers, or rates of pay). Where documentation is not available, different oral accounts of the same event can sometimes be compared for consistency. This can be especially convincing when accounts given from opposite sides of a conflict agree on the events and issues involved. Often, however, we have to rely on less convincing evidence, such as the internal consistency of details given within one account.

Much of oral history relates to one person's experiences, and this is usually a good thing. In fieldwork we learnt to ask people what had happened to them as individuals as a way of going beyond popular stereotypical notions of, for example, relationships with neighbours or the role of women. Good history comes from using these individual accounts to develop hypotheses about wider social relations, which can be tested against other case studies. The really 'slippery' part of history is not the raw historical testimony, but what it means. The meaning of all history is constantly changing. For example, we look at what happened in the 1920s in a different way than people did in the 1930s, because we know that the Second World War was one of the long-term outcomes of what had happened then. The best we can aim for is a historical account, which from our own point of view, we cannot go beyond.

Irish people are sometimes said to be trapped by history, but the fascination of the subject is not only its horror stories, but the rich evidence it provides for human ingenuity and generosity. In the following chapters, we will try to use the approach to history outlined above to examine relationships within farming families, ties with neighbours and hired workers, and some of the ways all these have changed. This will allow a discussion of the notion of community, a sense of belonging – whether it is anything more than a nostalgic fantasy, and why it is important for country people today.

Chapter 2

The family

THE NOTION THAT ECONOMIC SYSTEMS change is part of modern popular culture. Many people are aware that systems such as capitalism, communism, feudalism etc., differ in terms of who controls property and labour resources, and the ways in which commodities are defined and exchanged. Marxist theory, in particular, emphasises these differences and the social revolutions that brought them about. However, it was a Marxist, John Berger, who pointed out that in contrast to all this upheaval, in farming, relationships between land and labour can be remarkably unchanging. A farm holding worked by a family is one of the most widespread and long-lasting economic arrangements in the world. Berger saw this as central to defining 'peasant' societies, and the key to their survival.

> Their implements, their crops, their earth, their masters might be different, but whether they labour within a capitalist society, a feudal one, or others which cannot be so easily defined, whether they grow rice in Java, wheat in Scandinavia, maize in south America, whatever the differences in climate, religion and social history, the peasantry everywhere can be defined as a class of survivors.[1]

It would not be possible to discuss the history of farming life in Ireland during the last three centuries without including family ties, and the way these ties were used to ensure the family's survival (Fig. 6). Families had two main roles in this; at most times, in most places they provided the core of the labour supply required to work the farm, and they created the channels through which land could be passed from one generation to another.

Of course, when we look at Irish family farms, we find a lot of diversity within the overall structure just outlined. One of the good results of the new Irish histories and local studies of recent decades has been an increased awareness of this complexity, and the role of families in apportioning land, and keeping control of their holdings is a clear example of the differences that can be identified. The range of relationships involved includes the negotiations within extended kin groups who shared many rundale settlements (Fig. 7), the

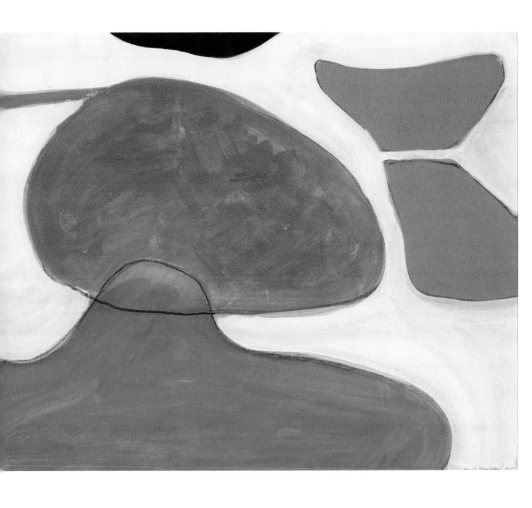

5 'Mayday. Thugamar Féin an Samhradh, Linn', by Philip Flanagan, gouache on paper (2004).

6 For almost 300 years, mixed farming was common in most of Ireland, the range of crops and livestock including potatoes, oats and barley, and cattle, pigs and poultry. Successful farms produced food for home consumption, and for sale. (Photo: Lawrence coll. R1786, National Library of Ireland.)

consolidation of holdings on family-run commercial farms (Fig. 8), and the games of power politics played out by Anglo-Irish kin groups. No historical account could give an accurate, full account of the range of these and other relationships. However, we can highlight some key aspects of family life that affected the inheritance of land generally, and the organisation of work on most farms.

One of the points that we will emphasise repeatedly in the book is that bleakly 'realistic' accounts of life on family farms are no more 'real' than the positive, sentimental views they aim to debunk. When we look at Irish rural family life in the light of both popular and scholarly evidence, we can develop a model which, if incomplete, does help us to go beyond the myths and polemic of some 'nativists' who describe how families functioned in rose-tinted romantic terms, and some 'realists' who look for meanness and manipulation everywhere.

7 Rundale group, Machaire Clochair, Gaoth Dobhair, County Donegal, *c.*1880. Rundale was a system of joint landholding that allowed very poor people access to strips of arable land, and communal grazing. Most Irish landlords saw the system as inefficient, and as giving rise to disputes. Most tenants valued the close neighbourly ties created by joint decision-making, and intense social interaction. (Photo: Glass coll., courtesy Trustees, National Museums Northern Ireland.)

8 A prosperous farming family, the Danaghers of County Limerick, 1905. Commercially successful farms, especially in Leinster and Munster, were quick to adopt new implements and techniques. The marketing of crops and livestock became more centralised and efficient, especially after the construction of railways in the 1850s. (Photo: Irish Agricultural Museum.)

Patriarchy

Irish family farms were, and largely still are, male dominated. The extent to which this is true appears in all sorts of ways, including how fathers and mothers are addressed. In places as far apart as Counties Down, Wexford and Galway, for example, we have heard the father referred to as 'the Boss', and the mother as 'Mammy', terms that clearly distinguish between the father as the key authority figure and the mother as a nurturer. The accuracy of this distinction is confirmed by many accounts, and field observations of farm operations in the recent past. The father, who was almost always also the farmer, made all major decisions about both planning and carrying out farm work. This exercise of authority shaped his relationship with his sons, sometimes making it noticeably formal, and potentially antagonistic. The American anthropologists, Arensberg and Kimball, summarised the situation as they saw it in County Clare in the 1930s.

> A son working on the farm's entire day-to-day activity, particularly in farm work, will be with his father … This fact colours greatly the relationship of father and son … There is none of the close com-panionship and intimate sympathy which characterises, at least ideally, the relationship in other groups … In its place there is developed … a marked respect, expressing itself in the tabooing of many actions, such as smoking, drinking, and physical contact of any sort … everything in the behaviour developed in the relationship militates against the growth of close mutual sympathy. As a result, the antagonisms inherent in such a situation often break through very strongly when conflicts arise.[2]

Some anthropologists have suggested that the father's power on many Irish small farms derived from the system of inheritance, which was often not one of primogeniture, but one where the father chose one of the sons to succeed him.[3] John Messenger alleged that this was especially true on the Aran Islands in the 1960s, where he claimed that some fathers deliberately encouraged sibling rivalry.

> Tensions between fathers and sons develop in childhood and often later on flare into scarcely-repressed hostility, especially in families where competition for inheritance of property is engendered among siblings by their fathers to ensure favourable treatment in old age.[4]

9 Father and son working together. There were sometimes deep tensions between fathers and sons, arising from both everyday decision-making, and the eventual inheritance of the farm. There were also vital shared interests in the farm's survival and development. (Photo: Green coll., courtesy Trustees, National Museums Northern Ireland.)

Messenger claimed that this typically led sons to hate their fathers,[5] which, if true, must have distorted life on the Aran Islands in disturbing ways. Fortunately, Messenger's negative view is unconvincing for several reasons, the most important being the limited extent to which siblings actually wanted to inherit the farm at the time Messenger was writing. In case studies of land inheritance on small farms in Counties Donegal and Galway in the 1960s and earlier, the choice of an heir was not a carefully negotiated procedure, but an uncontroversial result of the working out of the family life-cycle. In these case studies, it was found that the eldest son often inherited the farm because being the eldest, he was likely to be the first of the siblings to learn farming skills (Fig. 9). However, in a significant number of cases, the youngest son inherited, not because of any special skills or commitment, but because he was the only one left, his older brothers having emigrated. On Hornhead in north Donegal, for example, people talked of 'getting away' from the land, and of others who 'had to come back' from Scotland or England because there was no one else to look after the farm.[6] By the 1960s, farm numbers in the Republic generally were declining at a rate of 2.5% a year because young people were attracted by higher wages paid in urban areas. In County Cavan, Damian Hannan found that the movement away from the land was especially marked in small farms because of a fall in status of small farmers.[7] In 1976, Sacks reported that land was being sold in County Donegal because the heir did not want it.[8] All of this suggests that while a vicious father might be able to stir up rivalry between his sons on profitable, larger farms, it would have not been an effective strategy on Aran in the 1960s, where Messenger describes most the farms as subsistence holdings.

The power exercised by the father in choosing which son should inherit a farm would have been more obvious in earlier periods when land was desperately needed to ensure food supply, but this did not necessarily mean conflict within families. Fathers would have had a particularly decisive role in apportioning land at the poorest end of the social scale, in areas where subdivision was practised in the nineteenth-, and in some places well into the twentieth-centuries. We could also expect strategies for inheritance to be highly developed on large commercial farms, and the estates of the landed gentry. On many of these, primogeniture seems to have been applied, but literature and drama of the period, both English and Anglo-Irish, is full of fears, hopes and conspiracies related to wills. In these situations, fathers who were so inclined could behave tyrannically. However, it would be unconvincing to claim that this created a determining context in which Irish fathers automatically behaved as tyrants. The strategies and moves of the players described in the literature often produced unexpected results, which is why it still attracts modern readers.

Clearly not all Irish fathers were tyrants, and even in situations where fathers were brutally oppressive, that was not the whole story. One of the grimmest accounts of the relationship between an Irish father and his children was written by John McGahern in the 1960s. *The Dark* is, among other things, a story of parental violence and abuse on a small farm in County

Leitrim. The description of the children gathering potatoes dug by Mahoney, their father, conveys the oppressive tension.

> Between the lone ash trees, their stripped branches pale as human limbs in the rain, Mahoney worked. The long rows of the potatoes stretched to the stone wall … and they had to set to work without any hope of picking them all. Their clothes started to grow heavy with the rain. The wind numbed the side of their faces, great lumps of clay held together by dead stalks gathered about their boots.
>
> Yet Mahoney would not leave off. He paid no attention to them. He had reached close to the stone wall and he was muttering and striking savagely with the spade as he dug …
> Then they saw him come, blundering across the muddy ridges.
> 'Give me the bucket in the name of Jesus. Those bloody spuds'll not pick themselves.'
> He heaped fistfuls of mud into the bucket with the potatoes, in far too great a rush, and the bucket overturned and scattered his picking back on to the ridge. He cursed and started to kick the bucket.
> 'Nothing right. Nothing right. Nothing ever done right. All lost in this pissin' mess.'[9]

However, because McGahern is such a fine writer, even in this brutal novel, light does sometimes get through. The complexity of the father and son relationship is made clear when they work together making hay.

> Haytime came, the blades of grass shivering on the tractor arm, the turning and the shaking, its dry cackle against the teeth of the raker, the constant rattle of the teeth down again on the hard meadow after lifting free. The fragrance of new hay drenched the evening once the dew started and they were building high the cocks. Joy of a clean field at nightfall as they roofed the last cocks with green grass and tied them down against the wind.
> The smell of frying bacon blew from the house as they finished, hay and hayseed tangled in their hair and over their clothes as they walked towards the house, a gentle ache of tiredness. They shared something real at last. They'd striven through the day together, the day was over. No thought or worry anywhere, too tired and at peace to think.[10]

10 'Small imitations of their fathers'; boys at a fair in Castlewellan, County Down, *c.*1915. (Photo: Green coll., courtesy Trustees, National Museums Northern Ireland.)

'Realist' accounts which present all Irish farmers as tyrants in their own homes are no less romantic than the rosy claims they aim to counteract, albeit expressions of a more gothic, dark romanticism. Like almost all societies past and present, Irish farming society was and is controlled by men, but Irish fathers could be as affectionate and loving as any father.

> Only last week, walking the hushed fields
> Of our most lovely Meath, now thinned by November …
> I went unmanly with grief, knowing how my father,
> Happy though captive in years, walked last with me there …
>
> For that proud, wayward man now my heart breaks …
> Who curbed me, scorned my green ways, yet increasingly loved me.[11]

The relationships between Irish farmers and their sons were as complex and wide-ranging as those between any human beings. These relationships may have been expressed at the deepest levels, as budding farmers' sons learnt from and imitated their fathers from an early age (Fig. 10). Rosemary Harris affectionately described the behaviour of small boys at Ballygawley fair in County Tyrone in the 1950s.

> It was essentially a man's world … Perhaps it would be more accurate to say that it was a man and boy's world, for many of the farmers kept their sons away from school to help them in the Fair, and they came in, small imitations of their fathers, with sticks in their hands and serious expressions, their minds on cattle and not on larking about.[12]

Mastering the necessary skills was part of a development that eventually led to a son taking his father's place. If some Irish farmers behaved as tyrants to their sons, some sons played a complementary role, of the ambitious, impatient heir apparent.

The Irish mother

> I love the dear fingers so toil-worn for me,
> God bless you and keep you, Mother Machree.[13]

In contrast to the stern, authoritarian father, the dominant stereotype of the Irish mother is one of a doting parent, who is doted on in return (Fig. 11). The place of the mother in Irish popular culture is remarkable. In 1971, Big Tom McBride, 'The King of Irish Country Music', produced a record of greatest hits (Fig. 12). Of the ten tracks, five deal with mothers – four of them dead, or very old. The pain of losing one's mother is the main recurring theme:

> Some children take a liking to their parents,
> While others fill their mother's heart with pain,
> But some day they will be sorry for their blindness
> When the crying will not bring you back again.[14]

While the emphasis in many songs and poems is on the relationship between mothers and sons, the love of daughters for their mother was also the subject of a lot of emotion, real and sentimental. 1950s' ballad singers such as Bridie Gallagher and Eileen Donaghy praised mothers effusively, and 'the Queen of Country', Philomena Begley, rivalled Big Tom in her expressions of devotion.

11 A mother and baby near Clogher, County Tyrone, *c*.1906. (Photo: Rose Shaw coll., courtesy Trustees, National Museums Northern Ireland.)

> If there's medals for mothers,
> Mamma you'll win every one.[15]

The anthropologists, Arensberg and Kimball, saw a big difference in relationships between mothers and sons, and fathers and sons in 1930s' County Clare.

> The [mother, child] relationship is the first ... into which a child enters. It is very close, intimate and all-embracing for the first years of life. ... [The mother] is both guide and companion. Her authority most often makes itself felt through praise, persuasion and endearment ... If the child must leave the farm for other walks of life ... In exile, the bond lingers as a profound sentimental nostalgia.[16]

This statement could apply to almost any human society, but the extent to which it is dwelt on in Irish popular music is probably exceptional. The Irish mother has the special place shared with Jewish mothers, Polish mothers and Italian mothers – that of a self-sacrificing saint.

Of course not all Irish mothers were doting and self-sacrificing martyrs. The Anglo-Irish mother in Molly Keane's *Good Behaviour* is icy, vicious and manipulative, while the mother in Patrick Kavanagh's *The Great Hunger* is full of malice.

> Poor Paddy Maguire, a fourteen-hour day
> He worked for years. It was he that lit the fire
> And boiled the kettle and gave the cows their hay.
> His mother, tall, hard as a Protestant spire,
> Came down the stairs bare-foot at the kettle-call
> And talked to her son sharply: 'Did you let
> The hens out, you?' She had a venomous drawl
> And a wizened face like moth-eaten leatherette.
> Two black cats peeped between the banisters
> And gloated over the bacon-fizzling pan.[17]

12 Big Tom and the Mainliners, Greatest Hits album. Five of the ten tracks have the word mother in the title.

However, Poor Paddy Maguire's mother is memorable because she is so unusual. Social anthropologists and writers are right to emphasise the contrast between the father as the source of authority and discipline, and the mother as providing warmth and intimacy.

Whatever its source, the Irish mother's emotional power is still formidable. In the 1990s, a friend of ours was teaching in a secondary school in County Derry when corporal punishment was stopped. We asked him how he kept control in a classroom of 15-year-old boys, without the sanction of a smack or slap. He said it was simple. 'They all have mammies. You just bring them outside the door and ask them, "What would your mammy say if she knew you were behaving like this?" That is the end of it.'

Marriage

In classic anthropological studies, marriage is seen as a system where women are exchanged in marriage by men, to create alliances, or increase wealth and status (Fig. 13).[18] Katherine Tynan, writing in 1909, bluntly described such a situation in the south and west of Ireland. 'The prospective bride is bargained over with no more sentiment than if she was a heifer.'[19] The provision of dowries, claimed to be widespread in rural Ireland until well into the twentieth century, was part of the exchange. As late as 1957, the cash prize competed for by women at the National Ploughing Championships was a dowry of £100. (Two women shared the title 'Queen of the Plough' that year, but since neither got married within the next twelve months, the prize was not awarded.)[20] Rather than a relationship between lovers, marriage was an economic arrangement. Romantic love is one of the main themes of Irish songs and poetry of the last 300 years, but for all the passion expressed in great love songs such as 'Donal Óg', most marriage alliances involved detailed, pragmatic calculations.

Arranged marriages, or 'matches', became more common in the decades after the Great Famine of the 1840s.[21] The negotiations were sometimes facilitated by matchmakers. The extent to which a matchmaker (basadaeir) had a formal role in arranging marriages varied with time, place and the affluence of prospective partners. In the Lough Gur district of County Limerick, it was claimed that the daughters of respectable farmers were supervised so strictly that but for the matchmaker there would have been no

13 A bride attended by straw boys in County Sligo, 1920. (Photo: Green coll., courtesy Trustees, National Museums Northern Ireland.)

marriages, and as late as the 1960s, John Messenger claimed that most marriages on the Aran Islands were arranged, with 'a match-making ceremony' marking the end of family negotiations.[22] The matchmaker, usually a man, might work voluntarily, or be paid, but the overall evidence for how marriage negotiations were organised is often fairly impressionistic. Caoimhín Ó Danachair, who had many years' experience working with the Irish folklore archives in Dublin, concluded that rather than calling in a matchmaker, it was more common for the parents or friends of the young couple to meet at a fair or market, and then to go to the back room of a local pub to thresh out details.[23] The aim of the negotiations was to match the man's land, cattle and other resources, to the woman's dowry (spré), or 'fortune'.[24] Around 1900, it was claimed that dowries passed to the father of the groom, who would use it to help some of his other children to emigrate, or to make up a dowry for one his own daughters. There was often too little money to provide dowries for all daughters. Joanna Bourke claims that in a typical household of six children, two daughters would be unable to marry. Even when resources were sufficient to provide a dowry, matches were often made difficult by disparities in wealth, and opposed by calculating parents. Ó Danachair claimed that one gap too wide to be crossed by marriage was that between a farmer's daughter and the son of a landless labourer.[25] The situation was frequently referred to in traditional songs and ballads.

> I know I'm no match for her, not in the least, with her house and two cows, and her brother a priest![26]

More cheerfully, there are also plenty of examples of parents successfully conniving to secure a good match.

> Johnnie get up from the fire, get up, and give the man a sate,
> Don't you know it's Mr Maguire and he's courtin' your sister Kate!
> Ach, you know he owns a wee farm a little way out of town.
> Get up out of that ye impudent brat
> And let the man sit down![27]

More cheerfully still, the most famous instance of an arranged marriage in Ireland, that of Mary Kate Danaher (Maureen O'Hara) and Sean Thornton (John Wayne) in the film *The Quiet Man*, shows the whole arrangement to be driven by love, and also by Mary Kate's 'mercenary little heart' (Fig. 14).

> *Mary Kate* [the bride-to-be]: What did Sean … say about my fortune?
> *Michaleen* [the match-maker]: He says he doesn't give a sh… He says it's all one to him if you come in the clothes on your back, or without them.
> *Mary Kate*: Oh, he did, did he? Well, a fine opinion he must have of me, if he thinks I'd go to any man without my fortune … I'd have you tell him, that I'm no pauper to be going to him in my shift! … Until I've got my dowry safe about me, I'm no married woman. I'm the servant I've always been.

Mary Kate clearly had a major say in her marriage negotiations, but this was not always the case. A number of accounts stress how little the marriage partners might know one another. The alleged incident described in one story we heard in County Leitrim illustrates how this could be carried to extremes.

14 How it should have been. Marriage negotiations between Mary Kate Danaher (Maureen O'Hara) and the matchmaker Michaleen O'Flynn (Barry Fitzgerald) in the film *The Quiet Man*.

A farmer married a local girl that he hardly knew. After the wedding he approached a group of girls standing outside the church. 'Whichever one of you I married, will you come on home. The cattle need milking!'

At their best, arranged marriages involved negotiations that recognised the need to ensure economic well-being, but that also took the feelings of the prospective partners into account. The celebrated County Kerry writer, Peig Sayers, did not meet her husband before her wedding was negotiated, but the match was spectacularly successful. She was told of the potential match by her brother in Dingle.

> 'Cad é an sceal é?' arsa mise.
> 'Scéala cleamhnais, a chailín!' ar seisean.
> 'A Dhia na bhfeart! Cé hé an fear?' arsa mise.
> 'Fear ón Oileán', ar seisean. 'Buachaill mín macánta, agus fear maith leis. Tá súil agam go ndéanfaidh tú rud orm. Beidh said ag teacht chugainn oíche eígin.'[28]

'What news?' I asked him.

'News of a match, my girl!'

'God above! Who's the man?'

'An Islandman', he said, 'An even-tempered, honest boy and a good man as well, so I hope you'll take my advice. They'll be coming to visit us, some night soon.'

Things moved quickly.

> Three nights after this, three [Blasket Island] men walked in the door. They got a hearty welcome. My father had no idea that they were coming but then he realised fully what had brought them. After a little while one of the men produced from his pocket a bottle with a long neck; … bottle followed bottle … I didn't open my mouth … I couldn't decide which of the three was asking for me … Each one of them was too good a man for me … Oh dear, that match didn't take long to make! … I had two choices in the palm of my hand – to marry or go into service [as a maid servant] again. I was sick and tired of that same service and I thought it would be better for me to have a man at my back and someone to protect me, and to own a house of my own.[29]

Peig was fortunate. She loved her husband very much. They had ten children, five of whom survived. Not surprisingly, this kind of happy outcome was not always guaranteed. At their worst, arranged marriages were very unhappy. One County Cavan woman in such a situation claimed that the day her husband died was the happiest in her life.[30]

Whether or not arranged marriages are successful is still a major issue in some societies globally. Happily, there is plenty of evidence for warmth and love in Irish rural families, no matter how the marriage was agreed. Two sisters brought up on a small, commercial farm in Gannoway, County Down, remembered their father's love for their mother, expressed in exchanges such as, 'I think I'll go up and see how the corn is doing. Are you coming with me?' 'Sure we were up last night.' 'Aw, come on up anyway.'

By the 1950s, there is plenty of evidence that many marriages were the result of rituals of courtship, which are still well-known in the Irish countryside, rather than the result of negotiations between kin groups. The strategies and sad compromises adopted by the characters in William Trevor's celebrated short story 'The Ballroom of Romance' still show a concern with making a good match, but the calculations were made by the men and women involved, not by their families.[31]

Worldly realism suggests that love and poverty cannot co-exist, but this, happily, was not always the case. The American missionary and do-gooder Asenath Nicholson travelled around Ireland in 1844, just before the Great Famine. She described the kindness she received in a cabin near Urlingford, in County Kilkenny. A bed had been made up for her in one of the cabin's two rooms.

> A bed, fixed upon chairs and made so wide that two could occupy it; and [the woman of the house] … assured me that so glad was she to see me, that she would sleep in part of it by my side. It was certainly an extension of civility to leave the good man … His bed was made of a bundle or two of straw, and a decent woollen covering put over it.

> Never had I been placed where poverty, novelty and kindness were so happily blended. I fell asleep, nor did the barking of a dog, the squealing of a pig, or the breathing of a man, woman or child arouse me till I heard, at sun-rising, 'Well Maggie, how are you this morning? D'ye know I was lonesome without you?' 'God be praised', responded the good woman, 'and I hope you are well, Johnny.'[32]

Bachelors

> I'm livin' in Drumlister
> An I'm getting very oul'
> I have to wear an Indian bag
> To save me from the coul'.
> The deil a man in this townlan'
> Wos claner raired nor me,
> But I'm livin' in Drumlister
> In clabber to the knee.[33]

The Great Famine of the 1840s convulsed Ireland in the short and long-term. The long-term effects were very obvious in the decimation of the Irish population. Before the Famine, Ireland had a rapidly expanding population, people marrying young and having big families. For more than a century after

15 Joe Kane of Drumkeeran, County Fermanagh. In 1920, at the age of 7, Joe was sent to live with an unmarried uncle. He looked after his uncle in his uncle's old age. Joe believed that to do anything else would have been 'very ungrateful'. He inherited the farm in 1953, and lived there alone for the rest of his life.

the Famine, the country's population decreased, and people got married at much older ages. By the time of the First World War, the average age for marriage had risen to 33 for men and 28 for women.[34] For reasons we will discuss below, women left the land in much greater numbers than men, and this led to the phenomenon of the Irish bachelor. In the early twentieth century almost a quarter of farmers over 55 years old were single. The situation was even more extreme on small farms (under 6.1 hectares), where more than 60% of older farmers were single.[35] Hugh Brody reported that in Inishkillane by the 1960s, a household was frequently made up of either old people alone or bachelor children who stayed on the farm to save their parents from a lonely and helpless old age and the land from abandonment (Fig. 15). 'The young who remained at home used to inherit a farm, but today they inherit more isolation than land.'[36] Brody identified a link between this isolation and depression. Twelve out of 231 households had people suffering from mental illness associated with isolation and depression. A district nurse who visited Inishkillane once a week claimed that she gave out more anti-depressants than headache tablets.[37]

Around the same time that Brody developed his model of decline in the west of Ireland, the Irish Farmers' Association pointed out that an aging population had direct, negative implications for farming practice throughout the Republic. Large amounts of land were in the hands of people who were not receptive to innovation, and, the Association alleged, would put obstacles in the way of younger people who did want to innovate.[38] In part, the negative impact of bachelor-run farms was simply due to problems of labour supply. In the next section we will outline a model of the division of labour within small- and medium-sized farms. This 'ideal type' model was based on a family unit of two able-bodied men and a woman. Holdings farmed by bachelors were obviously one of a number of farm types where this model did not apply.

Hugh Brody summed up the situation in 1963: 'The bachelors of the communities are potentially the most depressed group … Many of these men have accepted their life in duty to ageing parents' wishes rather than in any enthusiasm for the kind of life entailed in remaining on the land and they see little future in the life they have been obliged by circumstances to endure.'[39]

The apparently inexorable decline of the west was dramatically interrupted by the impact of Ireland joining the European Union, and the 'Celtic Tiger' phenomenon during the decade around the new millennium, when land values rocketed and large numbers of people moved into areas previously seen as places from which to escape. The long-term effects of the recession years following 2005 remain to be seen.

Farming families at work

On the vast majority of Irish farms during the last three centuries, most labour has been provided by family members. This was especially the case on farms of up to 30 acres of arable land in the western counties of Mayo, Leitrim, Galway, Roscommon, Clare and Donegal.[40] Oral testimonies are consistent that at busy times, or where there was a shortage of labour because of sickness, death, or there were no children, any member of the family could be expected to carry out whatever work was necessary. This meant that sometimes even young children were required to do work normally carried out by adults (Fig. 16). For example, in 1920, at the age of 7, Joe Kane of Drumkeeran, County Fermanagh, was sent to live with his unmarried uncle. Joe's uncle couldn't cook, so the young Joe asked a neighbour woman to teach him. By the age of nine, he was an accomplished bread maker.[41] Childhood was not seen as radically separated from adult life in the way it is commonly perceived in modern urban life. In County Tyrone in the 1950s, Rosemary Harris found that

> farmers … wanted children because their help was usually essential to the economic running of the farm … Children on all farms began to help from the time they were about six. On the smaller farms particularly, children rarely 'went to play' with anyone except their own brothers and sisters … boys passed into their teens still anxious to learn more of adult farming techniques from their fathers.[42]

During the era when horses were the main source of power for heavy farm work, before 1955, the skill boys were most anxious to learn was working with horses (Figs. 29 and 80). Joe O'Neill of Dungiven, County Derry, began to learn to work with horses when he was about 8 years of age.

> When I came home from school, my older brother [might be ploughing, and] … he'd let me hold the plough. The Ransome's [wheel plough] was easy enough to hold, you know, and [it was also easy to] make the horses go out square, so that they wouldn't get over the chains … [I learnt] bit by bit … until finally he'd be away somewhere to look at something else, and I'd plough maybe four or five furrows … He showed me how to make the horses pull the plough … The horses less or more knew anyway.

A neighbour also taught Joe.

> I don't know whether I'm a very good ploughman or not, but I got a very good schoolin'. We had a neighbour, Micky Fearron [one of the local blacksmith's family] … It was him that showed me how to make a back and how to make a hint … He'd see me and he'd come over to me from [his own] … farm.

Bob Lee, of Cloverhill, County Cavan, learnt to plough when he was 13 years old. He said that neighbours would watch his attempts and comment gleefully on mistakes.

16 Children working in a bog. In the early twentieth century, children began to help with farm work when they were around 6 years old. Before the 1920s, some children as young as 7 were hired as farm servants. (Photo: Museum of Country Life, National Museum of Ireland.)

17 A boy pounding whins (furze) for fodder.

In them days, a man going past… would stop and look to see what kind of ploughing [had been done. If he thought it was poor, he'd say] … 'What kind of hokin' match did he make here?' And if you did make a hokin' match, you'd hear about it! And that would be some morning maybe at the church gate, when there'd be a dozen people about or something like that! And you wouldn't like that now!

The Lees had a wheel plough, like the one used by Joe O'Neill, but Bob Lee also enjoyed using a swing plough, which was more difficult to use, but allowed very fine adjustments to the width and depth of the furrow turned. Many Irish farmers testify to the pride taken in carrying out a task as neatly as possible.[43]

There is some evidence that children on wealthier farms were given leisure to play with one another. Mary Carberry's memories of growing up on a 200-acre farm in County Limerick in the 1860s were of stories and treats from her nurse 'Dooley'.

When I think of home I see first Lough Gur, lying in summer sunshine … and four little girls playing ring-o'-roses before the door of their home, or touch-wood on the lawn.[44]

Even in this idyllic account, however, it was recognised that most children were also expected to work.

[After school, the] little scholars came home … by cow-time [5p.m.], so that they could help with the milking and carry the pails into the dairy for their mother. One brought in turf for the fire, another drove the cows into the fields, a third fed the pigs and shut them into their styes.[45]

Women's work

Tasks like those just mentioned could be carried out by both girls and boys, but in the adult world they were usually seen as women's work. However, women might also carry out work usually done by men. Working with horses was usually men's work, but some women worked with horses, especially on farms where there were no sons. Dolly and Isabel Lyons, for example, came from a family of four sisters on a farm in Gannoway, County Down. They worked with horses every day, and were skilled in all sorts of horse work, apart

18 William Lyons of Gannoway, with his daughters Dolly and Isabel in 1933. The girls worked with horses from early childhood.

from ploughing. Neither sister remembered having been taught to work the skills required. 'You were just brought up with them' (Fig. 18). (This also applied to other skills. Both women knew how to milk a cow before they started school, but neither could remember actually learning how to do it!) The Adams sisters, who lived on a farm at Lisbane, County Down, also helped their father with horse work, but their work with crops was more generally in line with tasks usually carried out by women. They helped in the hay harvest, forking drying hay or 'lapping'[46] it in wet weather. In the grain harvest they bound sheaves and stoked them. In the absence of men in the family, Grace Adams helped her father to make hay and corn stacks, and she and her sister Lily did some work with horses.

> We used the Tumblin' Paddy in the fields. Sometimes Grace drove the horses and I [Lily] tumbled the Paddy ... Sometimes sowing grain, I used to harrow it in. [We] never tackled the ploughing.[47]

It was rare for a woman to plough with horses. This is reflected in the Irish word for widow, baintreach, the roots of which are 'a woman who farms/

19 Hazel McMahan of Ballybranagh, County Down, grubbing potatoes in the 1940s. By the mid-twentieth century women were competing regularly in ploughing competitions, but Hazel was one of very few who ploughed with horses at home as part of everyday work.

ploughs',[48] one possible implication being that a woman would only plough if left alone in the world. Happily, the one woman we met in thirty years of fieldwork who regularly ploughed with horses on the family farm was Hazel McMahan (later Hazel Kelly) of County Down, who on one occasion ploughed a six-acre field on the family farm at Ballybranagh (Fig. 19). After ploughing, she still had enough energy to play tennis and dance to Glen Miller tunes at a local war-time dance in Ardglass.[49] By the mid-twentieth century, significant numbers of women were involved in competitive ploughing, with horses, and, increasingly, tractors. In 1954, the founder of the National Ploughing Association, J.J. Bergin, proposed that the national championship at Killarney should have a 'farmerette' class for 'Girls, single, married or widowed, without reference to age, the winner to be known as "The Queen of the Plough".' The new category was claimed to be a resounding success (Fig. 20).[50]

20 Queen of the Plough, Muriel Sutton, at the 1959 National Ploughing Championship, Kilkenny.

On a farm with a large, well-grown family, many tasks were clearly allocated by gender. In general, men were responsible for the heavy or skilled work associated with crop cultivation and care of livestock. Women often looked after smaller and younger animals, and also helped with crops, especially at busy times, such as harvest. Before the early twentieth century, however, their main responsibility was the processing of farm produce in tasks such as butter-making, bread-making, and the curing of bacon and ham.

(a)

(b)

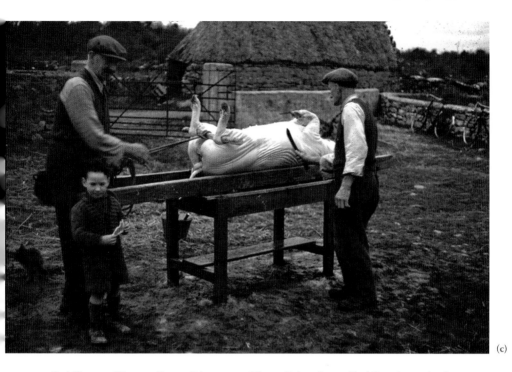

(c)

21 Pig killing near Kinvarra, County Galway, 1950s (Photos: Robert Cresswell). a) Preparing to slaughter the pig; b) Collecting blood from the newly slaughtered pig; c) Preparing to clean out the carcass. Food produced by farm women from pigs included ham, bacon, sausages, black pudding, haddock (stuffed pig's stomach), crubeens (pig's feet) and brawn (made from the pig's head).

Pigs and bacon

The importance of women's skills in processing farm produce, and their ruthless efficiency, is well illustrated by their work in the slaughtering and processing of pigs and their meat. All over Ireland, until the mid-twentieth century, pigs slaughtered for home use were usually killed and processed on the farm. On most farms, the farmer would help with killing the pig, a task that usually also involved a skilled local pig-killer (Fig. 21). After the dead pig had been gutted, and hung for a day (Fig. 22), the women took over, curing the bacon and hams, but also saving the offal – the heart, liver and fat. Pigs' feet, 'crubeens', were a popular source of meat, while meat sliced from the head was sometimes used to make brawn. The intestines were often stuffed to make sausages or black (and white) puddings, and the stomach might be used for tripe, or stuffed with potato, oats and pork scratchings to make an Irish version of haggis.[51]

22 Hanging a newly slaughtered pig's carcass at Loughinisland, County Down, in 1919. (Photo: McNeill coll., Down Museum.)

23 Both men and women milked cattle, but it was usually seen as a woman's task. Girls often learnt to milk before they started school. (Photo courtesy Trustees, National Museums Northern Ireland.)

24 Butter making. On many farms, butter was made once a week. Women would sell or barter any butter not needed for home use. (Photo courtesy Trustees, National Museums Northern Ireland.)

Butter and eggs

At the end of the nineteenth century it was found that in the west of Ireland, income from butter-making, and the trade in eggs, along with money earned from home industries such as knitting, meant that women were often making more money than men.[52]

Women had clearly defined tasks in the care of cattle. Before the spread of milking machines in the 1950s, cattle were milked twice a day by hand (Fig. 23). Milking one cow could take about ten minutes. Some of the milk produced was made into butter, one of women's biggest contributions to farm income. On small farms with one or two cows, butter or cream was stored in an earthenware crock and churned one day a week (Fig. 24). Women could sell or barter excess butter, which was one of Ireland's biggest farming exports. However, around 1900, there were concerns about its quality.[53] Apart from the

ARCADE. NEW TIPPERARY.

25 Butter market in the arcade at Dillon Street, Tipperary, *c*.1890. A number of purpose-built butter markets appeared in provincial towns during the nineteenth century, especially in the rich dairying regions of north and east Munster. (Photo: Lawrence coll. T287K, National Library of Ireland.)

butter sold through Cork's Butter Exchange, the largest in the world in the late nineteenth century, there were few attempts to organise quality testing of butter (Fig. 25).[54] Butter was most plentiful in spring and summer, which meant that it was cheaper. Women and traders were tempted to hold on to home-made butter until prices were high, and because of this it was alleged that butter was often inedible by the time it reached urban markets. The establishment of creameries transformed the situation. The first creamery was opened in 1884, and by 1900 the co-operative movement had established 236 dairy societies throughout the country, with a membership of 26,577. The movement was particularly strong in the west, in counties Limerick, Tipperary, Kilkenny, Sligo, Cavan, Monaghan, Cork, Leitrim and Waterford (Fig. 26).[55]

26 Meadowvale Creamery, Charleville, County Cork. The careful placing of girls and women in the foreground of this photograph may have been for picturesque effect. It may also have been intended to suggest that women were committed to the work of creameries, something that co-operative leaders thought doubtful. (Photo: Lawrence coll., no. 10428, National Library of Ireland.)

Farmers who sold their milk to the creameries were said to have increased their profits by 30–35%,[56] so the establishment of co-operative and commercial creameries was a big success story – for men. Co-operative leaders noted the lack of enthusiasm of women for the movement, and soon realised that this was because the money for butter and milk production now went straight to men. The change occurred over several decades. In 1914, around 60% of butter was still made on farms, but the move to creameries continued. The co-operative movement was accused of pushing farm women towards emigration, an allegation strengthened by parallel movements in poultry-keeping.

The care of free-range poultry was regarded so much as women's work that country people we talked to during fieldwork were often amused at the notion that men might help with it (Fig. 27). Rosemary Harris summed up the position as she found it in County Tyrone in the 1950s:

27 Feeding chickens at Tartaraghan, County Antrim, *c*.1900. Even very small farms would often have a flock of around 100 chickens, and it was estimated that 40 chickens equaled a cow in value.

> Looking after poultry and turkeys was women's work essentially, and neither the farmer nor his labourers would have dreamt of giving a hand with it. Once [the farmer's wife] ... did ask ... the hired man to help her and he was furiously indignant – locally any male over about thirteen or fourteen would have considered himself insulted by such a request.[57]

Poultry have been kept in Ireland for almost 2,000 years, but the numbers of fowl expanded greatly in the late nineteenth century. By 1900, there were around 18.5 million chickens in the country, more than three times the number recorded in 1850. Even tiny farms in the west might have a flock of 100 birds, and it was estimated that 40 hens equalled a cow in value. In the south-east, and particularly in County Wexford, the production of table fowl was important, but even in this area, egg production was by far the major source of income. The income from the sale of eggs was huge. In Baillieborough, County Cavan, for example, it was claimed that women made more in one day by selling eggs than their husbands made in a week.[58]

The care of poultry provided an important reason for women to work with their neighbours, something more common between men. Mrs Ellen Gibson described the situation in County Down in the 1940s.

> There was no foxes then and the hens wasn't closed in at nights … If you saw a neighbour's hens out early in the morning, well [you knew] them was good layers. And you went along to see if the neighbour would gather you two settings of eggs [for hatching] … and you asked if she wanted them swapped, or did she want money … [In return for swapped eggs] you had to take your eggs [for eating], and you had to give her a day or two to pick them, because you didn't want a great big egg … because sometimes they would have died in the shell coming out.[59]

This account shows the close attention to detail and the practical knowledge that women brought to the egg business. As in the butter trade however, problems arose because of the system of collecting, grading and delivering eggs. These were recognised and discussed in the late nineteenth century. Again, as with the butter trade, eggs were most plentiful in summer, and prices were correspondingly low. Women, and the shopkeepers or egg merchants they dealt with, were tempted to keep eggs until prices improved, so that by the time they arrived in British industrial centres, it was alleged that the eggs were often inedible. Leaders of the co-operative movement began to encourage farmers to send eggs to the creamery, where they could be sorted, graded, cleaned and packed and shipped to markets quickly. In the early twentieth century, Ireland had a developed railway network, which facilitated transport of goods. Malachy McSparran of Cushendun, County Antrim, told us that when the local railway was functioning, eggs traded in the market in Cushendall could be sold in Liverpool the next day. This efficiency depended on the co-operatives' work, but many farm women disliked sending eggs to the creamery, where the money would be added to the milk account, and paid to the (male) farmer.[60] In the long run, women lost out. Door-to-door collection of eggs declined, shops stopped exchanging groceries for eggs, and the creamery or egg centre became the only large-scale outlets for eggs. By the mid-twentieth century, new intensive poultry farming methods such as the deep litter and battery systems meant that it became acceptable for men to become involved in large-scale poultry farming. As in butter production, these changes and this removal of control of production led to a long-term fall in status for farm women.

Irish country women were not alone in this. Damian Hannan described similar changes in Germany in the 1930s.

> [In Germany] the role of farm women became increasingly less satisfactory as the nineteenth and twentieth centuries progressed. Her age-old role as food and clothing processor dwindled in importance as participation in the market increased. However, this original role was replaced by increasing her share of farmyard work; feeding pigs and calves, milking cows … etc. Her jobs appeared to become 'dirtier' and more toilsome as more traditional roles declined … As a result, the stereotype of the farm woman with the 'black apron and wellington boots' has become powerful.[61]

The deskilling of women and their subsequent desire to emigrate were matched by the attractions of city life. Their new opportunities in urban life were celebrated in a rhyme quoted by Joanna Bourke.

> Where is the maiden all forlorn
> That milked the cow with the crumpled horn?
> She has gone to the town
> Where she's now holding down
> A job as a skillful typewriter.[62]

Even before their key skills were made redundant, women's situation on many farms was seen as grim. In an otherwise rose-tinted account of farming in County Limerick in the 1860s, Mary Carberry commented,

> In those days young girls had nothing to look forward to but a loveless marriage, hard work, poverty, a large family and often a husband who drank. Small wonder then that when they could they did escape to America.[63]

Since the Great Famine of the 1840s, three women have emigrated for every two men, and recent changes have done little to make farming more attractive to them.[64]

In the first decade of the new millennium, women played a key role in the development of small farms specialising in products such as local cheeses or organic vegetables, but on the vast majority of Irish farms, the distance between women and farm work has continued to increase. This was repeatedly emphasised by people interviewed during fieldwork in County Down in 2010, when everyone we spoke to said that most local women were not involved in farm work at all. Robert Maxwell, who has a farm near Ballyhornan, said that during the previous twenty-five years, almost all the farm wives he knew had taken outside jobs. His own wife is a professional child minder, and other farm women he knows are nurses and teachers. May McAdam, from outside Ballywalter in the north-east of the county, summed up the situation. 'There's hardly a farm you would go to that you'd be speaking to the farmer's wife – she's out at work.'[65]

Changes in men's work

Men's dominant role in running farms has not been diminished, but how they manage their land has changed radically. Ongoing consolidation of holdings means that farms in general are much larger than they were in 1900, but the numbers of farmers and farm workers has fallen. (In 1911, over half the male labour force in Ireland was engaged in agriculture. By 1981, this had fallen to under 15%.)[66] Productivity has risen, almost without any break, however, an achievement which has been possible because of mechanisation and the adoption of a 'scientific' approach to the use of fertilisers and other chemicals. The widespread use of contractors, instead of farm labourers, has made the farmer's work more managerial and to some extent less hands-on.

Mechanisation of crop production was closely tied to the use of tractors, and these were introduced very quickly, especially during the two World Wars (1914–18 and 1939–45), as farmers responded to government compulsory tillage policies. In 1917, when the Irish Department of Agriculture established a tractor section, there were only 70 tractors in Ireland. By 1918, there were 640. Henry Ford began to manufacture tractors outside Cork in 1917, and Harry Ferguson developed his world-famous, multi-functional tractors in County Down shortly afterwards. In 1939, there were only 550 tractors in Northern Ireland. By 1945 there were 7,300. In the Irish Republic, which remained neutral during the Second World War, there were fewer than half this in the 1940s, but by 1960 there were around 22,000 tractors in the south compared to around 9,000 in the north.[67]

In the first decade of the new millennium, crop production continued a long-term decline, and became more capital intensive, with tractors commonly costing more than 100,000 euros. Farmers began to rely on hiring contractors to do a lot of work that they had previously done themselves. Farmers had been familiar with this sort of arrangement since the 1850s, when it became common to hire a portable threshing machine to thresh all of the farm's grain in one or two days, but this type of once-a-year arrangement has now become an everyday one. By 2010, in County Down, for example, farmers reported using contractors for planting and harvesting grain and maize, cutting and baling silage and hay, and even tasks such as hedge-cutting. Farmers with suitable tractors and equipment often undertook some local contract work, while hiring outside contractors for major tasks. Large-scale contractors from the midlands and west of Ireland often began their harvesting work in the slightly earlier harvests in the east of the country, sometimes working during the night if the weather was suitable, using electric light.

The installation of electricity and mains water revolutionised rural living during the 1950s and 1960s, although the early impact of electricity was most obvious in domestic life rather than farming. Mains water had a huge impact on livestock farming, however. It largely removed the need to carry water to livestock in fields or in sheds, and farmers said that in some cases they could keep five or six times as many animals than they had before water was made available. In crop production, technology has reduced the need for farmers to employ labourers. However, some aspects of livestock farming can require labour inputs any time day or night. In the early years of the new millennium, the small number of men employed as farm labourers worked on farms specialising in livestock.

Irish involvement in the global economy of 'agribusiness' has become increasingly focused on beef and dairying; in 2003, most milk-processing in the Republic was controlled by three companies, and three other companies controlled the processing of two million beef cattle a year. Pork, lamb and grain production have also become centralised.[68] Ireland's membership of the EU has also had profound, ongoing effects on farming, leading to more consolidation, specialisation and bureaucracy. Commercially successful farmers have become financial administrators as much as skilled operatives, and family farms are increasingly seen as businesses rather than the foundation of a way of life. For the first time in history, the structural unit formed by a farming family and its land may become redundant, and as a class, the 'survivors' may no longer survive.

Chapter 3

The neighbours

Primitive communism?

DURING THE 1970s and 1980s, when the Northern Irish Troubles were particularly bad, some of us hoped that socialism would provide a way for people to see beyond the local tribal hatreds and ongoing atrocities. However, in Ireland, left-wing movements have remained generally small in scale, and often seem rather marginal. Marxist ideas can still give important scholarly insights into Irish rural life, but most country people do not seem to find socialist views either relevant or attractive. We once teased a friend in the Workers' Party about this, challenging her to tell us what her party would say to the small farmers of Ireland. She replied that her party wouldn't say anything to the small farmers of Ireland, they would just wait until capitalism had got rid of them! This of course was a joke, but it reflects a strand in Marxist thought, which views rural society as backward and doomed to extinction. Marx himself referred to 'the idiocy of rural life',[1] and compared small farmers in nineteenth-century France to potatoes in a sack.

> Smallholding peasants form a vast mass, the members of which live in similar conditions but … their mode of production isolates them from one another … Their … smallholding admits of no division of labour … and no variety of talent, no wealth of social relationships. Each peasant family is almost self-sufficient … A small-holding, a peasant and his family; alongside of them another peasant and another family … In this way the great mass is formed … much as potatoes in a sack form a sack of potatoes.[2]

The metaphor is clear enough, if rather insulting, but it ignores very important aspects of rural life. In the last chapter, we outlined the complex division of labour and associated skills within farming families, and Marx also seemed unaware of the important ties that linked farms with their neighbours, relationships that expressed a very highly developed sense of community.

28 'The Fragrance of New Hay Drenched the Evening', by Philip Flanagan, acrylic on linen (2012).

We have seen that Marx was right to emphasise the relative independence of farming families. It seems to have been a central aim for most farmers to make their family economically self-sufficient, living off the holding's produce and depending on no one for help. On small- to medium-sized farms, where the farmer and his wife were in good health, and where there was one grown-up son, very little outside help was needed for farm work. However, in the event of sickness or death, or at busy times such as harvest, farmers would call on their neighbours for help. The relationships of mutual help that resulted were known by special names, an indication of their importance. 'Comhar', 'neighbouring' or 'morrowing' were the most common terms for a working arrangement involving two neighbours, while 'meitheal', 'gathering', 'boon' or 'fiddler' referred to a group, which often had up to twelve members, and occasionally many more.[3]

Neighbours could be asked to help with almost any task.[4] Particular individuals were known for their skills. Some of these were apparently simple, for example, sowing grain by hand, which involved scattering it over the

29 Sowing grain broadcast, *c*.1920. (Photo courtesy Trustees, National Museums Northern Ireland, WAG 262.)

30 A bothóg in Gaoth Dobhair, *c.*1890. (Photo: Glass coll., courtesy Trustees, National Museums Northern Ireland.)

ground (Fig. 29). However, as with many manual techniques, sowing grain seed evenly actually requires a lot of skill. Throwing grain on the ground is obviously easy. Throwing the seed so that it is spread evenly over the ground surface is not. The late Cormac McFadden from Roshin in north Donegal told us that in the 1930s, several local farmers would ask one neighbour to sow their corn. He had a technique of hurling the seed at the ground, which made it bounce and spread evenly, something that became obvious when the plant shoots began to appear.[5] Neighbours would also undertake much larger-scale projects, such as house-building. The most dramatic instance of this kind of work we recorded was also reported from County Donegal, on Gola island. A young couple left the island in the morning to get married on the mainland. When they returned that night, the neighbours had built them a temporary dwelling of a type known as a bothóg (Fig. 30). They boiled a pot of potatoes in the newly made hearth, and celebrated the wedding with a céilí in the bothóg.[6]

In the 1930s, the American anthropologists, Arensberg and Kimball, were in no doubt of the importance of neighbourly help (which they called 'cooring') in Luogh in County Clare.

This co-operation is woven deeply into the countryman's habit and sentiment … The small farmers of Luogh explained their co-operation in their own general terms. They call it 'cooring' in the brogue. The word is the Irish comhair [comhar], meaning aid, partnership, and alliance. They explained their 'cooring' in terms of the 'friendliness' of the place … they 'had right to help their friends', or in a more general statement, 'country people do be very friendly, they always help one another.'[7]

Tensions and conflicts

It is clear that neighbourly help was widespread, and often essential, but if we accept that most farmers prefer to be economically independent, we have to consider whether working with neighbours was something farmers did reluctantly, and whether it led to tensions. Arensberg and Kimball belonged to a school of anthropology that saw society as a well-oiled, self-adjusting machine, a view that treated conflict as unusual and short lived. However, they recorded a beating where a man was seen to be failing in his obligations, and they also concluded that in County Clare in the 1930s, continued failure to provide neighbourly help would result in 'social death'.[8] When we look at the kinds of work that required neighbours to help one another, it is clear that there were situations when we might expect tensions to arise, and there are plenty of instances where this was the case.

Weather in Ireland is notoriously changeable. In a bad season, there might be only a few days in which tillage or harvest can be carried out. In this situation, where tasks had to be completed as a matter of urgency, tensions arising over which neighbour got the work done first would not be surprising. Concerns that the amount of help given and received was fairly balanced in the longer term might also be expected. Tensions and concerns such as these were recorded most commonly when farmers lent or borrowed horses. In 1802, for example, Richard Thompson reported that in County Meath,

> [where farmers were] obliged to join before a plough can be made up, these plough alternately, and from the time they commence their operations, until the sowing is finished they are continually disputing about the work done; whose turn it is to have the united force next, and each accusing the other of making his horse work (harder) than he should, and (by tying up tight in the yoking and other petty contrivances) sparing his own.[9]

The same sorts of allegation were still being made in the 1930s. Mr Dan McKay from near Cookstown, County Tyrone, described the end of a 'morrowing' relationship with a neighbour for quite similar reasons. The incident began when he was ploughing one spring morning. He had only one horse, which meant that the ground had to be ploughed twice to turn it to the required depth. His neighbour saw him working, and offered to lend him a horse, to make up a two-horse team. As Mr McKay expected, after his own work was finished, the neighbour asked if he could have both horses to do his own ploughing.

> He wanted mine, and I couldn't say no. And he kept mine … at night. I says, 'Well I have this mare fed bravely … and … I don't want you to give her first grass hay – that's hay with the seed slapped off it … As you know yourself, it's no good for an animal that's fit to work.' [He asked that more nutritious upland hay, and some oats be fed instead.] …
>
> So he had my mare working for two or three days anyway, and I thought he should be bringing her home again … So I went down … It was after dinner hour, and I skited into the stable, and the stand that mine was in was crushed full of first grass hay, and the other one was clean, with some of the [good] upland hay, where his horse was standing. I wasn't in too good temper …
>
> [I met] the farm's servant girl in the yard and this girl said, 'Your mare is working bravely, this weather.'
>
> Says I, 'I suppose.'
>
> 'Aye', she says, 'She was out here before seven o'clock these mornings. And more than that, them hen houses there … it was your mare that pulled them out … to the fields.'
>
> His own brother had big horses, and this man that helped him had big enough horses but they took it out of mine. So I wasn't feeling in too nice temper.
>
> 'Aw', he says, 'I'm glad you come. You'll need the mare home. I didn't know whether to send the girl up with her or not.'
>
> 'Ah', says I, 'I think if you had just brought her out to the roadside there … and turned the rope, she would have come home [on her own].'
>
> Says he, 'I'd like to get the corn in.'
>
> Says I, 'Well, I'll either sow it or harrow it … Will I bring the corn out and sow it, or what?'
>
> 'Aw', says he, 'Mary Ellen will carry it to me.'

He didn't want me to sow the corn, you see. He thought I mightn't do it right …

Says he, 'You can take the horses.'

Says I, 'I suppose I could.'

So I got the horses in anyway, and got tea, and a good feed of corn for the mare … She had more than she could bear …

[When it came to adjusting the harrows, I saw that] the swingle tree was lying on the fair … If he had been a decent man, I would have turned it over and let mine get the short one, you see and done the heavier bit [of pulling]. But, says I, 'We'll just let him get a swing of his own.' … So [my horse] … was a big number anyway, and his was a tight wee thing and I … gave him a wheen of belts along the side …

So when he was done sowing, I had the harrowing finished … The sweat was running out of … [his horse, and as far as I was concerned, he could] stay all night to soak in it! And I got the mare up the road … and gave [her] more to eat and let her go to bed. So that finished the morrowing with him.[10]

Tensions arising over lending and borrowing horses were widely recognised. One farmer in Swillybrin, in north County Donegal, wryly summarised the situation: 'If you kept the horse too long, they accused you of laziness. If you brought it back too soon, they said you'd been overworking it!'[11]

Sometimes, neighbours fell out for even more striking reasons. One dramatic incident was alleged to have occurred in the Rosses in Donegal in the 1930s.

There was three men on Cruit island, and they used to help each other in springtime … cutting the seaweed [for fertiliser] …

So this day … they were coming in with a cargo of wrack, and the little boat they'd with them went on a rock … Well this lad went in to shove her off the rock … And he shoved her off – he was hanging on to the side of her you see. And one of the boys in the boat … thought the boat was going to capsize, and he got hold of one of the pins … for putting the oar in, and he started hitting him on the knuckles, telling him to let go of the grip. He said, 'Never again would I go out with them boys.'[12]

This was clearly a case of meanness brought on by panic, and it does not represent typical attitudes or behaviour. The weight of oral and written evidence emphasises that tensions and conflict were not the norm, and that kindness and generosity between neighbours were much more common. The late Bob Lee, who was brought up near Cloverhill in County Cavan, was clear in his assessment.

> You'd be reckoned a very awkward man, if a neighbour [asked you for help and you] … didn't fall in line with whatever [he wanted] – If you wanted to cut oats today or dig potatoes, and [the other man] also wanted to dig, well, you'd hang back – one or the other. 'Well, maybe it'll suit better to do it your way.' … I never knew of any nastiness in my life-time.[13]

Several people we discussed the subject with pointed out that tensions were often avoided because neighbours were familiar enough with one another's work to know when help was available, or required. In the early twentieth century, for example, a lot of grain on small farms was threshed with flails. This was part of the winter work routine, and could be postponed until both men were free. There was a generally expressed view that exchanges should be fair, that a day's work should be repaid with a day's work. Some people, such as widows, clergy, or invalids, were not expected to return help, but in other cases, days owed might be remembered for years. Around the time of the First World War, for example, Cormac McFadden of Roshin, north Donegal, was sent regularly to dig for a neighbour because this man had helped the McFadden family when the children were too small to work on the land.[14]

Groups of neighbours

Some farming work was undertaken by large numbers of people. For example, in Turlough, County Mayo, in the 1930s, neighbours would join together to thresh one another's grain (Fig. 31).

> Súiste a bhí acu leis an choirce a bhualadh … Is minic a bhí meitheal acu, ligeann siad síos ceithre punnanna agus bíonn beirt fhear os comhair a chéile ag bualadh.

> They used a flail to thresh the corn … Often they had a meitheal. They lay down four sheaves and there are two men opposite each other threshing.[15]

31 'Flailing'. This painting by Seán Ó Seadhacháin (1901–91) shows a group of men threshing with flails in west County Limerick. The large number of men is unusual. It was more common for two men to do the work. (Photo courtesy National Museum of Ireland.)

As we have just seen, this work could be fitted in as other winter tasks allowed, but in the uncertain Irish climate, having help from a number of workers for other tasks might be crucial. For example, a group of seven men digging a field in one day was not simply seven times faster than one man digging for a week. It might mean the difference between getting crops planted quickly, and not getting them planted at all, if the weather turned bad (Fig. 32).

Sometimes, large-scale machinery might also require inputs from a number of workers. For example, mobile threshing machines, hired out for a few days, became very common after their introduction to Ireland in the 1850s. These required 12 to 16 men to operate them properly, and the work teams were commonly made up by a meitheal, or 'gathering', of neighbours

32 Harvesting potatoes, County Galway, *c.*1900. (Photo courtesy National Library of Ireland, CLON 739–4.)

(Fig. 33). Most one to one working relationships in farming work were between men, but women were frequently part of large groups recruited for planting or harvest, and women had a key role providing food for working groups, especially at harvest.

There were different ways in which groups of neighbours might be recruited. Hugh Paddy Óg Ward, of Keadew in the Rosses, County Donegal, remembered arrangements in the 1920s and 1930s.

> They called it a 'fiddler', because there'd be a dance that night, maybe in … the house they had gathered in to dig the ground. And there would be a lad would come and play the fiddle… I mind my eldest brother … called a fiddler … I think it was after St Patrick's Day … There was a lot of digging to be done … and he got thirty-six spades digging … but in later years, I mind a lad up the road … took badly, and we said we would gather, you know, and dig the ground for him, but there were only four or five of us came. And that finished it. That would be now, about the outbreak of the [Second World] War.[16]

33 A group of haymakers in County Tyrone, 1906. (Photo courtesy National Museums Northern Ireland.)

Sometimes, however, neighbours would just turn up to help. Mr Dan McKay remembered one incident in County Tyrone.

> One day the neighbours come to me, and I had potatoes [to dig and gather] ... I had given the neighbours a whole lot of plants – cabbage plants – and one day didn't four of them come with spades to dig for me. And I had to gather for them all! [He found this painful, because of a weak hip] ... They had come to dig and I couldn't very well say, 'Come you boy, and gather!' They were doing me the favour and I had to do the best I could to keep it moving. There be's some good neighbours to morrow with ... and some would want to use you.[17]

As with arrangements between two farmers, notions of fairness applied when people exchanged help. In larger groups, it was often simply measured by days worked, but here also, the obligation to return help could be postponed, or even set aside entirely. In the 1950s, in Columcille, County Longford, for example,

It was very common for a meitheal to gather for a man that would be sick and couldn't do his own work. The neighbours would gather and sow his oats for him or save his turf. The same thing was always done for a widow woman. They were not under any obligation to pay back anything. Often if a man had no horse to do the spring work, the neighbours that would have horses, five or six of them would go to that man with their horses on a Sunday morning, about four or five o'clock in the morning and do the work for him.[18]

Similar arrangements were reported in Seskinan, Decies, County Waterford, in the 1940s.

Bhí nós in san gcontae seo chun prátaí agus coirce a bhaint agus a shábháil don té ná beadh slí aige féin chun san a dhéanamh. Bhailíodh buachaillí óga an bhaile le héirí lae ar maidin Dé Domhnaigh, agus bhíodh an obair déanta acu roimh an Aifrinn. 'Meithil Mhaidean Domhnaigh' a tugtaí ar an meitheal sin.

There was a custom in this county to save the potatoes and corn for the person who was unable to do the work himself. The young boys of the place used to gather at sunrise on Sunday morning and the work was done before Mass. That meitheal was called the 'Sunday morning meitheal'.[19]

Big farmers

Neighbourly help was particularly associated with small farms. If we accept that people helped each other because they needed help themselves, this is not surprising; better-off farmers needed less help. In County Clare in the 1930s, it was claimed that the only wealthy farmer in the 'Luogh' district did not co-operate at all with his neighbours.[20] Most accounts, however, did include descriptions of participation by bigger farmers in exchanges. The wealthier man might not come to work himself, but would send a labourer, or lend a horse, or an expensive piece of machinery, such as a reaping machine or a tractor. The late Joe Kane from Drumkeeran, near Ederney, in County Fermanagh, had no horse, but needed the use of one to comply with government demands for more tillage during the Second World War.

34 Lint pulling, McSparran farm, Cloney, County Antrim, *c*.1943. This flax pulling 'boon' was made up of farm workers and neighbours. (Photo courtesy the late Malachy McSparran.)

> The like of me that had no horse … I'd go to my neighbour, maybe Jim Moohan … and he'd come for a day [with his horse] … and I'd give him two days of a swap.

Some farmers did say that exchanges like this could be used by wealthier farmers to their advantage. The anthropologist Peter Gibbon has argued that this undermines the notion of neighbourly help creating community solidarity. Any exchange between a big and small farmer would be arranged on the big farmer's terms, and serve to strengthen his social position.[21]

There is some evidence of distinctions made between people, based on wealth and status, at social events. Joe Kane described eating arrangements for a meitheal of men at a threshing day's dinner.

> The older type of man [and men who provided horses and carts], they were taken away to the [good] room, and there was a fowl killed, and the bottle of whiskey was up there … It was a kind of honour … The servant men and the working men [went into the kitchen] … and sometimes … if the man was anyway generous, he might give bottles of

stout to the ones in the kitchen – and sometimes they didn't get any drink at all … There wasn't much counted on the working man that time, you know.

It does seem that aspects of mutual help might have been used to reinforce differences in status, but it would be wrong to try to reduce all exchanges to hard-nosed economic calculations. The McSparran family, substantial farmers from Cloney, near Cushendun, organised groups of neighbours to pull flax on the farm or to help with threshing grain (Fig. 34). In this part of County Antrim, such a group was known as a 'boon'. The late Malachy McSparran said that the neighbours' help was repaid by allowing them the use of the McSparran's pedigree bull. The family had a saying, 'It's the bull that pulls the lint [flax].' Malachy was able to name all 29 people in a photograph taken during flax pulling on the farm in the 1940s. These included farmers, labourers, relatives, and some people who just came to enjoy the day. Occasions like this were clearly times when ties between people were celebrated and strengthened.[22]

Socialising

Far from being a chore, or an occasion when social tensions came to the surface, days when neighbours came together to work in groups were often times when celebration was intense. In the 1790s, the atmosphere at one such gathering organised to dig potatoes surprised the French traveller De Lactoyne.

> Men, women and children sang, accompanied by one or other kind of instrument … For the occasion the peasantry had put on their best clothes; the air of gaiety and good humour which showed itself among them would have made any spectator believe he had arrived on a fete day.[23]

Most accounts emphasise how enjoyable working groups could be, especially during harvest, or turf cutting. Joe Kane described a meitheal for moving haystacks: 'Ach, it was a kind of pastime, you know … There used to be a big day putting in the haystacks – They'd have bottles of whiskey, do you know … They were the greatest haystacks ever made! … You had no bother getting help if you produced the bottle of whiskey!'[24] In some cases, the festive element of

35 Binding oats, Gola island, County Donegal, *c.*1950. (Photo courtesy Coiste Forbatha Ghabhla.)

the meitheal led to complaints that they were more of a nuisance than a help. One account, collected in 1963, in Tisarain, Garrycastle, in County Offaly, was particularly dismissive.

> There was nothing only meitheals for turf-cutting and a dam' bad way of cutting turf it was too, with some working and more doing nothing.[25]

Another account, collected in 1958, in Aughmagree, Ballintober South, County Roscommon, also dismissed the meitheal system as a nuisance.

> The meitheal ... was more of a nuisance than anything else. Half of them would come to drink the porter and do no work. It was a case of too many cooks spoiling the broth.[26]

However, there is also plenty of evidence for well-organised work groups that completed the given tasks efficiently, and also ensured that people had an enjoyable time. Part of the enjoyment could come from the work itself. In an interview recorded in 1986, Bob Lee from the Cloverhill area in County Cavan, described the friendly but intense competition that might arise between workers. He gave an example of six spadesmen working together in a field.

> [You wouldn't be working very long before] … you would be trying to see if you could pass me. Quietly, you know – and maybe you'd be a better man at the spade than me, you see. Or you might be better than him. And whoever would get out first with their ridge or whatever they were doing, then they were reckoned to be the best. But there'd be somebody else who would be bound to try before night to see would he pass him by.[27]

In 1943, Michael Cardiff from Erris, County Mayo, described a situation where necessity and fun combined in what could be seen as the ideal meitheal (Fig. 35).

> As the reaping of the ripe corn was a work requiring expedition, as apart from any adverse weather, over-ripe grain automatically dropped to the ground, and was lost, reaping meitheals of men and women often were held. Such parties were scenes of cutting competitions as well as of fun and merriment, and at the close of the day, there was a dance and singing. In fact, an air of enjoyment and happiness seemed to pervade the atmosphere among the rural community during the harvesting season.[28]

Céilís

Socialising was an integral part of neighbouring. A meal, frequently followed by dancing, was often organised for the working group after their tasks were completed, especially at harvest time (Fig. 36). These occasions were common in most parts of Ireland. They were known by a number of names:

Camp	(Longford)
An chuinneog	(Donegal)
Churn	(Antrim, Armagh, Derry, Donegal, Down, Fermanagh, Tyrone)
Clabhsúr	(Cork, Kerry)
Féilséaras	(Galway)
Fiddler	(Donegal)
Harvest dance	(Kilkenny)
Harvest home or supper	(Donegal, Down, Kilkenny, Leitrim, Mayo, Monaghan, Westmeath, Wexford)
Head	(Carlow and Wexford)
Milséara	(Galway)
Punch dance	(Down)
Reaping dance	(Cavan)
Stampy party	(Limerick)[29]

36 Stampy party, County Limerick, 1907–8. A harvest celebration. Stampy was made from grated potatoes and seasoning. (Photo courtesy National Library of Ireland.)

37 A céilí (*Illustrated London News.*)

Working together also led to other kinds of socialising. One meaning of the Irish word comhar (a working relationship between two farmers) is 'friendliness', and people who worked together would also socialise together, most commonly at a céilí (Fig. 37). 'Cayleying' was much more informal than a harvest meal or dance, and usually involved a number of local men meeting in a house for gossip, card-playing, storytelling, and sometimes dancing, and drinking tea or alcohol. Joe Kane described how it worked in his home area of Drumkeeran, County Fermanagh.

> I used to céilí in Willie Jones's. Willie lived over in Gortgeeran but he left at the time of the War … They were all great musicians … There used to be great nights in it, there'd be fiddlin' and dancin'. Then the 'upper house' they called it, that was his uncle and aunt. They lived farther up the lane. They were great musicians too, and there used to be a lock of neighbours round … there used to be maybe nearly a dozen, and they'd get up and dance to the music. There were other houses we used to céilí in too … They'd be playing cards … they might be playing

for something – they could put up a rooster or something like that …
and there'd be tea, and there'd be a jolly night.[30]

Despite the possible tensions, and some evidence of meanness and re-
enforcement of status differences, the socialising that went along with
neighbourly help suggests that it brought people together in complex and
positive ways, not recognised in Marx's 'sack of potatoes' metaphor, or in social
theories that postulate economic strategies based on hard-nosed calculation.
People helped one another out of necessity, but often found the process
profoundly enriching.

Decline

Since at least the 1930s, there have been claims that neighbours do not help
each other as much as they used to. One reason commonly given is that young
people nowadays (whenever nowadays might be) have become selfish,
disrespectful and careless. This sort of complaint goes back at least to the time
of Socrates. In County Clare in the 1930s, the younger generation gave rise to
'universal complaint'.

> 'Young people aren't what they used to be', said one old farmer in a
> general discussion of the golden age that was his youth. 'They spend
> money on fags, they have to be gambling every night, or else [go] to a
> dance, and if they happen to win a turkey they will nearly shake the
> house down [in their triumph]. There is no good in the country when
> things go on like this. In the old days a man used always be out
> repairing his stone walls, cleaning his land, or doing something. Now
> you can't get them to do anything unless you pay them.[31]

The claim that things aren't what they used to be is commonly made by elderly
people, and can often be a lament for their own lost youth, rather than an
objective assessment of social change. However, more convincing, pragmatic
assessments are also given. Decline in neighbourly help can be understood as
a direct result of the ongoing depopulation of the countryside. In many areas
there were fewer neighbours whose help could be sought. Hugh Paddy Óg
Ward of Keadew, County Donegal, whose memories of 'fiddler' working
groups in the area was described above, said that just before he emigrated in
1962, 'You would go outside and you wouldn't see a light'; this in an area

categorised as a 'congested district' in the 1890s. Depopulation in the west of Ireland was mostly due to emigration, but there and elsewhere it was also due to the ongoing consolidation of holdings as they were bought up by successful commercial farmers. In north County Down, for example, in 2010, one fairly typical farm of 300 acres occupied land divided into ten farms in the early twentieth century.[32]

The most common reasons given for decline in help in areas of commercial farming are the mechanisation of farming and the intrusion of cash into exchanges between neighbours. People tend to put a cash value on exchanges which, in the past, were assessed in terms of general relationships. One of the oddest, but very telling, examples of this was recorded in north Donegal by Hugh Brody in the 1970s.

> I know of two men in north Donegal who pay each other £1 a day for help in cutting turf. First one pays for work on his turf, then the next week the second pays the first for work on the second's turf. Inevitably they end up paying one another identical sums.[33]

This kind of calculation can be understood as part of the commodification of more and more aspects of life, which seems to go along with 'modernisation'.

The availability of labour-saving technology is by far the most common reason given for the decline in neighbouring. Occasionally, new technology actually led neighbours to help one another more, the hiring of threshing machines mentioned above being a clear example. As we have seen, up to 16 men were required to operate a threshing complex (Fig. 38), and in most cases the team of workers would be made up of neighbours. The threshing could often be done on a farm on one day, but as neighbours went from one farm to another, men might be away from their own farm for three weeks to a month, a major commitment of time at a busy season.[34]

In general, however, mechanisation has dramatically reduced the need for neighbours' help. The use of portable threshing machines was an early example of the use of contractors by Irish farmers. By the year 2000, and more recently, as we have seen in looking at changes within family life, contractors were being used for most large-scale farm work, and especially major tasks related to crop cultivation – ploughing, planting, cutting silage, baling hay, harvesting grain (with a combine harvester), harvesting maize, cutting hedges and disposing of slurry. Using contractors does away with the need to invest in massive pieces of machinery, or to employ labourers. In County Down in the new millennium, contractors might be hired from as far away as County Tyrone.

38 A threshing meitheal at Rice's farm, Saucetown, south Tipperary, 1944.

Another consequence of contract work is that it does away with the need for neighbourly help. In County Down, in 2010, some farmers still sometimes worked with neighbours, but this was often an affirmation of friendship rather than a practical necessity. Jim Watson, of Slans, near Cloghy, for example, was justly proud of one friendship that crossed the local sectarian divide.

> Religion never comes in to anything down here. My next door neighbour is not the same religion as me, and if I needed a tractor today, I'd go and ask him for it and he'd give it to me, even if somebody else was using it, and I'd do the same for him.

In general, however, people are clear that working ties with neighbours have declined, and this is often a cause for regret. Robert Maxwell of Ballymenagh, County Down, was clear that the local community had suffered because of the decline.

People are still very good neighbours, but we don't see them. One man we used to work with a lot – we still see him on the road – he used to help with the silage and the grain [and] I would have cut his silage and grain – we maybe only talk to him two or three times a year now, although he only lives two or three miles down the road. Things haven't changed for the better in that way.[35]

Finding ways to replace the perceived loss of community ties created by neighbourly help has been an ongoing concern for politicians and social activists. Most initiatives try to replace the old networks with more formal arrangements, such as the infrastructure of the 'rural civilisation' envisaged by early co-operators.[36] In the 1930s, Sinn Féin developed a policy for co-operatives, known as Comhar na gComharsan. The use of the word comhar in this initiative, and in the general co-operative movement, was an attempt to link modern co-ops to older working ties between neighbours, as this 'philosophy' was claimed to be 'native Irish as well as being co-operative',[37] but so far the ideals have not been realised. The co-operative movement has been very successful economically. This would have pleased at least some of the movement's early leaders, one of whom explicitly stated, 'We make no war on capitalists. We aim at being capitalists ourselves',[38] but there has been a relative neglect of the movement's social goals, something that has been observed in the development of co-operatives in many parts of the world.

Modern co-operation is not … a continuation of … ancient forms [of mutual help]. On the contrary, it arose just at the point of history when the ideas of mutual aid … were at their weakest, so that economic life was given up to unchecked competitive capitalism.[39]

In Ireland, initiatives at state level, and more recently by the European Union, have almost all been taken in the context of 'unchecked capitalism'. In the early 1970s, for example, attempts were made to encourage farmers to engage in 'group operations', as a way to raise financial returns, and reduce unit costs for participating farms. Examples that were suggested included co-operation between several farmers in the production of a commodity such as dairy produce, where several dairy herds would be managed as one enterprise, the complete amalgamation of several farms to form one enterprise, and the development of group contract enterprises, where the farmers involved would produce, for example, store animals, calves, or dairy herd replacements.[40] By

39 Harvest field at Lisbane, County Down, 1942. Lily and Grace Cooke with John Adams and Willie McKee (centre). (Photo: J. Cooke.)

1972, pilot schemes for Group Farming Projects were in place in the Republic of Ireland. These offered grants for buildings and equipment, and covered key staff costs for three years. Beet growers were organised in machinery syndicates and in some areas pig-producers were operating successful weaner and bacon marketing groups. An Irish Farmers' Association report was upbeat about the potential of this type of organisation.

> It has been argued that Irish farmers would not accept [the] discipline [necessary for operations] … of this nature – discipline which, it is said, amounts to a loss of independence. This has been disproved by farmers who are already working in groups.[41]

In Northern Ireland also, co-operation for profit was also seen as a key strategy in overcoming the inefficiencies in distribution and marketing caused by fragmentation of organisations within the Agri-Food Industry. One recommendation in a report produced by the Agri-Food Strategy Board in 2013 was that the industry 'must develop distribution hubs for transporting produce to market and … consider development of co-operative centres for the intake of raw material'.[42] This is something that co-operative creameries have been doing for over a century. The modern initiatives, however, are advocated in terms of economic returns, rather than social development.

In 2010, co-operatives were still very important in Ireland, particularly in dairying, where more than 90% of the market share in the Republic was controlled by co-op societies, but as with Group production generally, the notion that the movement had social and cultural aims is no longer central to strategy in these multi-national operations.

Co-operatives were just one way that concerned people (mostly outsiders) have attempted to deal with the sense of loss expressed by many older country people. Church groups, community centres and heritage initiatives have all, to a greater or lesser degree, tried to combat widely reported feelings of isolation and loss of local identity, but the necessary mix of social and economic ties, good fellowship, and a sense of ultimate meaning has so far proved elusive (Fig. 39). What has been lost has been best expressed in poetry, such as Patrick Kavanagh's evocation of a threshing day in County Monaghan.

From Tarry Flynn

On an apple-ripe September morning
Through the mist-chill fields I went
With a pitch-fork on my shoulder
Less for use than for devilment.

The threshing mill was set-up, I knew,
In Cassidy's haggard last night,
And we owed them a day at the threshing
Since last year. O it was delight

To be paying bills of laughter
And chaffy gossip in kind
With work thrown in to ballast
The fantasy-soaring mind
...

I'll be carrying bags today, I mused,
The best job at the mill
With plenty of time to talk of our loves
As we wait for the bags to fill ...

Maybe Mary might call round ...
And then I came to the haggard gate,
And I knew as I entered that I had come
Through fields that were part of no earthly estate.[43]

Chapter 4

Farm labourers and servants

Come all ye loyal heroes and listen now to me,
Don't hire with any master till you know what your work will be.
You'll have to rise up early from the clear day light of dawn,
Or you never will be able to plough the Rocks of Bawn

(Traditional)

AGRICULTURAL LABOURERS were an important part of Irish rural society throughout the eighteenth century, and by 1840 more than a million men were employed in farming. However, defining what we mean by the 'farm labourer' can be difficult. A labourer was someone who lived by doing manual work for other people, but in Ireland many workers also had access to small patches of ground on which they could grow food for their family. Even though they had to labour to make a living, these people would often describe themselves as farmers, to the frustration of some state officials. The historian David Fitzpatrick suggests that the best way around the confusion is to identify where most of a person's income came from; if it was mostly from labouring, then the person was a labourer.[1] Different types of farm worker can be identified using this sensible approach – cottiers, farm servants, migrant workers and day labourers – but these were not rigid categories. As with the general category of labourer, arrangements could be very flexible.

Cottiers

The cottier (or cottar, or cottager) system centred on the exchange of labour for land.[2] Sean Connolly has summarised the essential elements of the contract.

> In its most distinctive sense this meant a labourer paid in land rather than cash. The cottier received from the farmer a cabin, a small plot of land sufficient to raise potatoes for a family, and in some cases grazing or turf-cutting rights. His rent, though calculated in money terms, was set against days worked at an agreed wage. In the decades preceding the

40 'Lughnasa, the Beginning of Harvest', by Philip Flanagan, acrylic on linen (2012).

Famine, these contracts provided the cheap man-power on which depended the whole system of capital-poor but labour-intensive tillage farming.[3]

The labourer might receive a small amount of money as well as access to land, but in some cases he would have to pay the farmer money to get the use of land, as well as providing labour. The latter arrangement became more common in the decades just before the Great Famine of the 1840s, when increasing population pressure led to greater competition for land.[4]

Connolly's definition makes the connection between cottiers and crop production, so it is not surprising that the biggest concentrations of cottiers were found in the big tillage areas of Ireland. However, as early as the 1770s, the great agriculturalist Arthur Young also saw the cottier system operating in many other parts of the country as well. He also attempted to summarise the main elements of the relationships and exchanges involved, which he thought had 'probably [been] the same all over Europe before arts and commerce changed the face of it'. His summary agrees with Connolly's modern analysis, in emphasising that the most distinctive aspect of the system was that the cottier's labour was exchanged partly for money, but also, more importantly, for the use of a cottage and a patch of land on which to grow food for their families. The patch of land was most often one or two acres in size, a garden plot rather than a tiny farm.

> If there are cabbins on a farm they are the residence of the cottars, if there are none, the farmer marks out the potato ground, and the labourers … raise their own cabbins … A verbal contract is then made, that the cottar shall have his potatoe garden at such a rate, and one or two cows kept [for] him at the price of the neighbourhood, he finding the cows. He then works with the farmer at the rate of the place … a tally being kept … and a notch cut for every day's labour. At the end of six months or a year, they reckon, and the balance is paid. The cottar works for himself as his potatoes require.[5]

Overall, Young was ambiguous about the cottier system. He calculated the average cost to cottiers of producing potatoes and milk under the system, and concluded that

> It is evident, as far as merely charging goes, there is no oppression upon them which can ever amount to starving. [However] in particular

instances, where there is much inhumanity in the greater tenants, they are made to pay too high a rent for their gardens … I believe from what I saw, that such instances are not uncommon.[6]

The relationship between cottiers and the farmers who employed them could be tense. Cottiers were anxious to be kept on for more than one year, and this made them very dependent on the goodwill of their employers. Tenant farmers who employed cottiers could impose various restrictions on them. For example, in the decades before the Great Famine, farmers in County Cavan prevented their cottiers from keeping chickens, to reduce competition in the growing egg trade.[7]

Arthur Young pointed out that paying for labour by providing a 'means of living' was not in itself a bad thing. He recognised that payments in kind were often abused in England, especially where industrial labourers were given items such as bread, candles, soap, etc., because the complexity of the accounts allowed overcharging for goods provided. However, he argued that the provision of land for potatoes and a cow was clearer and meant, among other things, that cash resources would not be wasted, as when monetary wages were used to buy whiskey.[8]

Young seems to have agreed with opinions he recorded in Johnstown, County Wexford. The tiny size of cottiers' holdings was not seen as a problem, rather it was the system of letting that should be changed. 'There is no objection to cutting off the cottars from a farm, and making them tenants to the landlord … Nor is there any doubt but out of them a race of little farmers might be gradually formed.'[9]

In 1793, the *Irish Agricultural Magazine* published an article which attempted to convince farmers of the desirability of providing cottages for their labourers, urging them in fact to increase the number of cottiers (Fig. 41). The advantages to be gained from this were summarised.

> The cottager is the main [labour] resource upon which the farmer can depend; if therefore he is fortunate enough to have several well-peopled cottages upon his farm, he will have little to fear from a want of hands on extraordinary occasions.[10]

By the mid-nineteenth century, however, the cottier system was disappearing. The Great Famine of the 1840s was decisive. Many cottiers either died in the famine, or emigrated. John Forbes, writing in 1852, saw the system's

41 'Digging the dinner, September 1894'. The tenancy of a cottage and access to a patch of potato ground in return for labour were the key elements of the cottier's lifestyle. (Photo courtesy Trustees, National Museums Northern Ireland.)

disappearance as a very good thing. He believed that it had 'debased' the mass of rural labourers in Ireland.

> However lamentable may have been the influences and the means whereby it has been broken up in Ireland, every well-wisher of that country must rejoice at its downfall. Through this system and its accompaniment – the grand element of its vitality, potato-food, – the people were debased to nearly the conditions of savage life. Secure of the means to maintain life and health by a minimum amount of labour, and in the absence of all stimulus to make them seek to rise above the low level to which they were born, they seemed to forget that man was a progressive animal, or had any nobler functions to fulfill, than to preserve individual life and to perpetuate the race … This form of Irish life … has been broken in upon, and may be regarded as in the process of being extinguished. This extinction, everyone will admit to be essential to the progress of the lower classes in Ireland.[11]

Forbes saw the long-term solution as creating opportunities for erstwhile cottiers (presumably the 'progressive animals' among them who had evaded 'extinction') to become small famers – a view that would be hotly contested at the time and since. In fact, most former cottiers who stayed in the country became day labourers, working for a weekly monetary wage. The terms cottar, cottier or cottager were often used in later texts, but the structural relationship between work and access to a house and garden was no longer present. In these later texts the terms were generally used to describe people who lived in a rented cottage with a garden. However, it is also clear that access to a patch of land where a labourer could produce food remained important.

Migrant workers

During the last three centuries in Ireland, many landless labourers, and farmers whose farms were too small to support a family, often worked away from home for part of each year. Numbers of seasonal migrants were relatively small compared to other farm workers, but their experiences captured the imagination of many country people and the resulting songs and stories are a major part of farming heritage (Fig. 42).

Seasonal migration has been documented in Ireland from at least the seventeenth century, but the number of migrants grew rapidly in the early nineteenth century, from a few thousand in 1801 to as many as 80,000 in 1845.[12] In the eighteenth century, most seasonal migrants came from commercially successful regions in east Leinster and south-east Munster.[13] However, in terms of the percentage of the population who engaged in seasonal work away from home, the migrants were most commonly from the west. By 1841, workers who travelled for work within Ireland, and those who travelled to Britain, mostly came from counties Mayo and Donegal. (5.2% of Mayo men, and 3.2% of Donegal men worked away from home for part of the year.)[14] Within these two counties, the numbers going away for seasonal work were concentrated in and around Achill Island in Mayo and the Rosses and Gweedore in Donegal. In 1881, for example, it was claimed that the majority of people on Achill Island in County Mayo simply locked the doors of their houses, sent their cattle to the hills for summer grazing, and set off in family groups to find work in Scotland.[15] In 1892, it was claimed that almost all able-bodied 'men, girls and children' in these areas worked as migrant labourers.[16] In Ireland generally, however, it was usually the men who went away.

42 Migrant workers leaving Achill Island, County Mayo. (*Illustrated London News*, 1880.)

(The 1841 census returns suggest that six times as many men as women went away from home to work.)[17]

In the late nineteenth and early twentieth centuries, attempts were made to estimate the overall number of migratory workers for Ireland as a whole. These figures are almost certainly an underestimate, but they do give a sense of the scale of the annual movement.

YEAR	NUMBER OF MIGRATORY WORKERS
1880	38,000
1890	23,000
1900	32,000
1910	18,500[18]

Seasonal migration made sense on tiny farms and conacre patches where potatoes were grown as the main subsistence crop. Weeding and moulding up a potato crop while it is growing increased the yield at harvest, but the women who stayed at home could do this work on many farms, and even where there was no care of the growing potatoes, a well-manured, well-drained potato crop would grow quite well. Going off to work as a migrant labourer was a way of dealing with the enforced idleness, or under-employment, found in many small farming societies. Cormac Ó Gráda has estimated that in the early 1860s, as many as 100,000 men migrated for seasonal work each year.[19]

Spalpeens (Spailpíní)

Most official enquiries into migrant labour in the last two centuries related to seasonal migrants who went to England and Scotland to find work, but others, generally known as spalpeens (spailpíní), travelled within Ireland to find work, often in spring or at harvest time. Official documentation of their movements would have been difficult. Anne O'Dowd suggests that generally, 'the workers simply took a chance and set out from home at the beginning of the harvest season when they knew that the farmers would be looking for extra hands for a few days' or a few weeks' work. In the south of Ireland especially the spailpíní, [also known as] cábóga and spealadóirí were drifters who wandered around on their own looking for work'[20] (Fig. 43).

Given the hit and miss approach of labourers searching for work, evidence of where men from any particular area went to is bound to be impressionistic. In 1893, a British Royal Commission recorded some of their movements.

HOME	WHERE WORK WAS FOUND
Cavan and Monaghan	Ardee, Co. Louth
West Donegal	Letterkenny, Strabane and Derry
Connemara	Loughrea, east Galway
Kilkenny	Roscrea, Co. Tipperary
Connemara, Leitrim, Longford and Cavan	Co. Dublin[21]

Farm workers and servants featured in many stories, songs and jokes. This is especially true for spalpeens, who are the subject of some of the most colourful songs and stories, and in the absence of detailed state and other records, these are an important historical source of insights into their experiences.

43 Spalpeen with a loy, drawn by William Harvey in 1850.

An Spailpín Fánach

Go deó deó rís ní raghad go Caiseal,
Ag díol ná ag reic mo shláinte;
Ná ar mhargadh na faoire am shuighe balla,
Um sgaoinsi ar leath-aoibh sráide…

Ní fheicfear corán am láimh chun bainte,
Súiste ná feac bheag rámhainne
Ach bratacha na bhFrainncach as cionn mo leapthan,
Is píce agam chun sáidhte

Never again will I go to Cashel,
And sell my health a-raking
Nor on fair days rove up and down,
Nor join the merry-making

You'll not see a hook in my hand for reaping,
A flail or a spade shaft
But the flag of France over my bed,
And a pike for stabbing.

Eoghan Rua Ó Súilleabháin

The most celebrated spalpeen poet was Eoghan Rua Ó Súilleabháin, who was born in the Sliabh Luachra area of County Kerry in 1784. Eoghan became a spalpeen at the age of 18, and spent the next ten years working either as an itinerant labourer, or an itinerant school master. There is no detailed record of his movements, or how he dealt with the practicalities of combining labouring and teaching. In 1924, Daniel Corkery attempted to imagine how it might have been.

> His wanderings have not yet been traced on any map … our only way of filling up this period of ten years is to think of him travelling the autumn roads with his spade on his shoulder, or as seated in a hut or by a farmer's hearth, a group of young men about him, all of them deep in the story of Ulysses, another wanderer.[22]

Eoghan Rua wrote two poems about obtaining a spade for digging, while 'An Spealadóir' (The Scythesman) deals with the poet's experience working as a mower, paid by the day.[23] These poems are part of a unique cultural heritage and an important source of information about cultivation techniques in the early eighteenth century. One of the spade poems is addressed to his friend Seamus, a blacksmith (Fig. 44).

> Forge me a tool, my Seamus,
> Fit for the earth,
> A well-tempered spade
> To work and till
> Clean furrows, welded
> To shape and hand-set.
>
> No sign of beating mar
> The press of silver steel,
> Loose and free with flexible
> Sweep and grain
> Of the wood-shaft tapered
> To regular borders,
> My tool will shine in the field.[24]

44 Spadesmen in Waterford, painted by Sampson Towgood Roch in 1824. (Courtesy the Trustees, National Museums Northern Ireland.)

Eoghan Rua lived up a stereotype which could fit either a particular kind of Irish poet, or a spalpeen, a fancy-free, drunken charmer. His rollicking career ended with his death in 1784, and he is probably buried in Killarney. The association of spalpeens with disorderly behaviour was so entrenched that the term came to be applied to any Irishman who was considered dirty, degraded or deprived.[25] This use of the term became very common in satirical articles and cartoons aimed at Daniel O'Connell's Repeal campaign.

In the early 1890s, researchers from the Congested Districts Board found that earnings from migrant labour were vital to household incomes in the west of Ireland.[26] However, from the middle of the nineteenth century there was a slow decline in crop production in Ireland, and this, along with increasing mechanisation, probably meant that the demand for short-term labour for spring work and harvesting declined more quickly than for other farm workers. By the end of the nineteenth century, spalpeens had moved from everyday life into folklore. More than any other group of labourers, the heritage they have left is one of poetry and songs.

Farm servants

Farm servants, like spalpeens, found work in Ireland, but can also be classed as migrant workers in that most of them worked away from home, sometimes a short distance, but often many miles. They moved less often than spalpeens as they were usually employed for a 'term' of work, which lasted for three or, more commonly, six months. Like spalpeens also, their terms of employment were well established by the early eighteenth century. For example, an entry in an inventory from Legecory, County Armagh, in 1717, reads:[27]

	s.	*d.*
First due to Danaill McClellen for one quarter's wages	6	6
2 due to Elinor Stevenson for halfe a year's wages	16	0

Farm servants usually lodged on the farm where they worked. This meant that they often lived very closely with their employers and the very intense relationships that sometimes resulted may be one reason why older country people who remembered the system were particularly interested in the subject.

Servants found employment in a number of ways. Sometimes the farmer and servant came from the same area, and knew one another as neighbours (Fig. 45), while other connections might be made by servants who were working away from home. These people could sometimes arrange contacts between potential masters in the area where they worked with people in their home area who were looking for work. However, most farm servants who were looking for work away from their own locality found it by going to a hiring fair (Fig. 46).

In England, there are medieval references to hiring fairs, and in Ireland there have been references to farm servants for at least 300 years, but so far we have not found clear references to hiring fairs before the early nineteenth century. In 1814, for example, it was noted that in County Tyrone, servants 'usually hire themselves to a farmer, but never for a longer term than six months at a time. There are two stated days in the year, when they assemble at Newtown Stewart for this purpose.'[28]

By the late nineteenth century, hiring fairs were very concentrated in Ulster, where they were held in more than eighty towns and villages. Hiring fairs of some kind were noted in more than fifty towns in the rest of Ireland, but only a few of these, such as those held in Dundalk and Drogheda, were as

45 Thomas Wilson of Letter, County Fermanagh, with the young man he hired, who became 'one of the family'.

organised on the same scale as the northern fairs.[29] The biggest fairs in Ulster were held in Newry, Strabane and Letterkenny. Most of the fairs were held around 12 May and 12 November; fairs in neighbouring towns were sometimes held on different dates, so that servants and farmers who were not successful in finding or filling a job at one, could try again at another within a few days.

46 'Derry Hiring Fair'. This painting, acquired for Derry Museums Service by the late Dermot Francis, shows the hiring fair in the city's Diamond around 1910. It is a rare illustration of servants carrying their bundles of belongings, and it is unique in showing a deal being struck by a farmer and servant.

Hiring usually took place in the town centre, often the main street or central square. Servants looking for work would sometimes identify themselves by wearing an emblem such as a stalk of straw, or by holding an implement with which they were skilled, such as a spade, sickle or scythe, but most were easily recognised by the small bundle of belongings they carried (Figs. 47 and 48). James Ennis, who was hired at a number of fairs in the 1920s, including Derry, Limavady, and Ballymoney, explained that it was easy to see who was looking for work.

> You had to have a wee parcel, you know, below your arm, and then they knew you were looking for a job … If you were well-dressed or anything … they didn't interfere. They'd look at you, a pair of oul' trousers with about ten holes in them, and … an oul' parcel … Even if you had nothing in the parcel, as long as you had [it] … they knew you were looking for a job. Sort of code, you know.[30]

47 Ballymoney hiring fair, County Antrim, 1906. This rare photograph shows servants, identified by the bundles of possessions they carry. It also shows how young some of them were.

48 Servant girl at Gortahork hiring fair, County Donegal, 1906. (Photo: courtesy National Museums Northern Ireland.)

Farmers would approach potential servants and negotiate terms and conditions of work, including board and lodging. Wages offered were based on the servant's experience, skill, and gender. Men who were skilled at working with horses were paid most, and women and boys, the least. Wages offered at Ballygawley hiring fair in 1894 show a typical range. 'Plough men received from £5 to £7 for the six months: boys £3 to £4 15s.: women £3 15s.: and girls £2 to £2 10s.: male and female "herds" 30s. to 40s.'[31] Accommodation and food were also discussed. Responses to questionnaires on the subject of hiring fairs make it clear that the quality of food given to servants was a key factor in their judgment as to whether farmers were good or bad employers, even more important than the hours they were expected to work.[32]

If a deal was made between a farmer and a servant, it was usual for the farmer to give the servant a small amount of money known as an 'earls' or 'earnest', which they could spend at the fair. The fairs could be colourful occasions, with trick-o-the-loop men, ticket sellers, singers, sheet-music printers, itinerant salesmen, musicians, full-time peddlers and fortune-tellers.[33] However, the hiring process is more often remembered with anger at what was seen as the degrading treatment of servants. For Patrick MacGill, the 'navvy poet' from the Glenties area of Donegal, Strabane hiring fair was 'the Calvary of mid-Tyrone', and 'the slave market'.[34] His description of the fair shows the antagonism between farmers and servants at these large events, where employers and employees were strangers to one another.

> We stood huddled together like sheep for sale in the market-place of Strabane … I felt tired and placed my bundle on the kerb-stone and sat down upon it. A girl … looked at me. 'Sure, ye'll never get a man to hire you if ye're seen sitting there', she said.
>
> A big man with a heavy stomach came up to me.
>
> 'How much do ye want for the six months?' he asked.
>
> 'Six pounds', I told him.
>
> 'Shoulders too narrow for the money', he said, more to himself than to me, and walked on.
>
> Standing beside me was an old father, who had a son and a daughter for sale. The girl looked pale and sickly. She had a cough that would split a rock … During one of these fits of coughing an evil faced farmer who was looking for a female servant came around and asked the old man what wages did he want for his daughter.
>
> 'Five pounds', said the old man …

'And maybe the cost of buryin' her', said the farmer with a white laugh as he passed on his way.[35]

Hostility between farmers and servants could erupt into violence. Men from Mullaghbawn in south Armagh, for example, were said to beat farmers who were seen as hard masters.[36] However, most violence at fairs seems to have been between the servants themselves. Drinking and fighting were the most commonly reported 'recreational' activities at all hiring fairs. At Comber, County Down, for example, servants would trail a coat behind them if looking for a fight. Patrick MacGill probably comes closest to making this violence intelligible. In situations where daily life was a grind of hard labour, he found that 'only in drink was there contentment, only in a fight was there excitement'.[37]

For servants looking for work, however, all these sources of excitement were very much secondary to the task of finding work. This was particularly true for the minority of young people who had no home farm to go back to. James Ennis, for example, who was born in 1910, and raised in Nazareth Lodge orphanage in Derry until he was 14, described being 'worried stiff'.

> You'd nowhere to go that night, unless somebody took you on, you know. Oh, you had to hire somewhere. You were tied, you see. There was no other jobs available at that time … It took you all day to get hired, for heaven's sake. You were running about here, and running about there … You've no idea what it was [like] getting hired. You daren't have moved from the Diamond [Derry's central square] for fear you'd miss a job. You had to stand there all day.[38]

Some servants, especially in east Ulster, lived at home, but most went to live on their employer's farm. The living conditions described in the questionnaire replies sent to the Ulster Folk and Transport Museum range from 'slavery' to being 'treated as one of the family'. A correspondent from Kesh, County Fermanagh, stated that 'in many cases the conditions were appalling as animals were kept better', while an account from Killeavy in County Armagh described conditions 'on a level with the employers'.[39]

Servant girls usually slept inside the farmhouse, some sharing rooms or even beds with the master's children. Allegations of sexual abuse of women servants were common. The true extent of abuse is probably unknowable, but the fear that girls might be abused may be one reason that fewer than a quarter of farm servants were girls.[40] Boys often slept in a converted outbuilding, usually a loft. If these were clean and reasonably furnished this suited some boys well, as in this arrangement meals were usually provided in the farm kitchen, and clothes were often washed by the farm women. In Scotland, where specially built bothy houses were often provided, men were responsible for cooking and cleaning with the result that the bothy system was associated with squalor and fighting. However, the provision of accommodation in an outhouse was no guarantee of good living conditions. One retired servant from Clogher in County Tyrone recalled,

> I myself was hired in a place and the first night I got a surprise as there were no furniture in the room except one bed and it was that old it must have come from Noah's ark and the bedclothes were nothing only rags.

In the worst cases reported, the servant boy's bed was simply a blanket or two thrown on the straw of a rat-infested barn.[41]

The quality of food given to servants was one of the basic criteria used in judging whether a farmer was a good or bad employer. On small farms (the preferred work place for most servants because they were 'friendlier'), the workers often ate the same food, at the same table, as their employers. On bigger farms, they would more often sit at a separate table, or even in a separate room, usually the kitchen. Even on tiny farms, however, farmers might find ways to mark the perceived status difference between themselves and their servants. When Paddy the Cope Gallagher was hired at the age of ten years of age, he sat on the floor to eat while his employers sat at a table.[42]

Patrick MacGill described how bad things could be.

> In the morning I was called at five o'clock and sent out to wash potatoes in a stream near the house. Afterwards they were boiled in a fire over a kitchen fire, and when cooked they were eaten by the pigs and me. I must say that I was allowed to pick the best potatoes for myself, and I got a bowl of buttermilk to wash them down. The pigs got buttermilk also. That was my breakfast during the six months. For dinner I got potatoes and buttermilk, for supper buttermilk and potatoes. I never got tea in the afternoon. The Bennets [his employers] took tea themselves, but I suppose they thought that such a luxury was unnecessary for me.[43]

However, he was treated much better on another farm.

I lay abed every morning till seven, and on rising I got porridge and milk, followed by tea, bread and butter for breakfast. There was no lack of food.[44]

Hours worked do not seem to have been a major matter for dispute. Most servants were the sons of small farmers, and this would have made them aware that many tasks had to be done, irrespective of the time taken. The large number of jokes, proverbs and anecdotes related to the ingenuity with which farmers made tasks for servants from early morning until late at night show the widely held perception that most farmers were determined to get as much work out of their servants as possible.[45] James Ennis, who was hired on a farm near Ballymoney, County Antrim, in the 1920s, said that he had very little social life, especially at busy times in spring. He described his employer as 'a fine man to work to', but one who was determined to get as much work as possible out of his employees.

This boy that was hired along with me in that place … we were at a dance in the town hall … and I looked at the watch. Says I, 'Hey, we'd need to run. Four o'clock!' Says I, 'We'd need to run if we want to get an hour's sleep'. And out we goes, and we'd bicycles, you know. Ten minutes it took us or less. We jumped on the two bikes and away like hell. And we met the farmer in the yard! 'Did you feed the horses yet?' – by the way he thought we were only rising! I was no' in the yard hardly. 'Man, that's great!' he says, 'Throw them horses a bite, ye boy ye!' … That was shortly after four o'clock in the morning. Man, I was raging, I didn't run far that night![46]

Growth and decline of hiring

We do not have a record of the numbers of young people who went to hiring fairs, but around 1900 the railway system was reaching the most isolated areas in the west, enabling young people to travel faster and further in the search for work. Seán Beattie estimates that 10,000 young people from Donegal became migrant workers of some sort in the early 1890s. From Gweedore alone 950 went to hire.[47] This may have been the temporary reversal of a national trend, as by this time overall numbers of farm workers in Ireland were decreasing dramatically. There are several possible reasons for the apparent anomaly.

Servants were usually hired to fill a gap in the family labour supply. These gaps might arise because of sickness, emigration or death, so the need to fill them could arise at any time. Also, while the long-term swing from tillage to pastoral farming during the period meant that fewer workers were required overall, there was an ongoing need for live-in workers who would be available to tend livestock at any time.

However, hiring did begin to decline. Between 1881 and 1911, live-in farm workers disappeared most rapidly from Connacht and Ulster. This was part of an overall change in the structure of farming, and also a reflection of concerns related specifically to the hiring system. There was a powerful movement to end child labour in all areas of work, and the removal of very young people from hiring was reinforced by the introduction of a minimum school leaving age of fourteen in the Irish Free State in 1926. New welfare provisions also reduced the need for older people to go into service. Numbers of adult servants declined sharply after the introduction of unemployment benefits in Northern Ireland in 1937. Servants no longer had to depend on their employer for food and lodging, and farmers no longer felt that they had to keep servants when work was slack.

In 1938, a committee appointed by the Ministry of Agriculture found that

> At many centres … the Hiring Fair is now little more than the occasion of public holiday … The decline has been closely associated with the development of weekly engagements … It appears that the small or medium farmer probably finds that a system of weekly engagements is more suitable for him. On such farms the need for employment all the year round is less great than on a large farm, and it appears that with the recent upward tendency in farm wages, and the advent of the scheme of unemployment insurance for agricultural workers, there has been a growing tendency for farmers to discharge men at the end of harvest and to re-engage them in the spring.[48]

The last hiring fair we know of was held in Milford, County Donegal, in 1945, although the employment of workers for six-month terms probably persisted in a few instances until the 1970s.

49 Hiring as slavery. Letterkenny hiring fair re-enactment, 2011. The caption accompanying this photograph on the internet reads, 'Actors depict the father striking a deal to hire out his daughter Niamh for a six-month employment period for £3 to a wealthy farmer. She would have to sleep in the barn under the straw and the first duty of the day would be to have the farm's eight cows milked for 7a.m. for collection to the creamery'. (Image copyright, Kenneth Allen.)

Commemoration

Re-enactments of hiring fairs have been held in a number of centres including Letterkenny in County Donegal, Ballyclare in County Antrim, and Strabane in County Tyrone. An educational project in the Ulster Folk and Transport Museum in the 1990s included re-enacting a fair, and dramatising the experiences of young servants, using farm buildings in the outdoor museum.

There is a noticeable difference in emphasis between the models of the past presented in the western and eastern re-enactments. At Letterkenny (Fig. 49), the suffering and ill-treatment of servants was emphasised, a theme also taken up in a poem about Derry Rabble (Hiring Fair).

Ah say there young Willie
D'ye think ye'll stay on?
Of course I will sor, till
The first Rabble morn.
It's then that I'll show you
A clean pair of heels,
For I'm sick to the teeth of your stony oul' fields …

If those were the good days,
Thank God they are gone,
When people were pledged
Like a coat to the pawn.[49]

In contrast to this, the Ballyclare May Fair reflects the nostalgic picture of hiring given in a poem by a retired servant from Larne, John Clifford, who, while recognising that there were some bad employers, lamented, 'Those golden hours, how soon they flee'. For Clifford, even the conditions under which unskilled labourers were employed revealed a wonderful harmony.

They get a bed, a bite to eat,
A dud o' claes, clogs tae their feet,
An odd half croon frae time tae time,
An' this arrangement works oot fine.

You'd nearly think some unwrit' law
Provided places for them a',
The way they fitted in sae weel
Like cogs in some great nick'd wheel.[50]

It would be easy to identify inadequacies in these models of the past, but to some extent they reflect historical reality. Oral and written testimonies are consistent that there were fewer tensions between masters and servants in small eastern fairs than in the bigger, more anonymous fairs held in west Ulster. At the eastern fairs, farmers and servants often knew each other as neighbours, and the hiring contract might be agreed outside the fair. In the west, this was more uncommon, and farmers and servants might view each other across a sectarian and linguistic divide, many of the servants being Irish-speaking Catholics, and the farmers English-speaking Protestants. From a northern perspective, it is always encouraging to hear generous testimonies which stress that people rose above sectarian stereotypes, and behaved decently to one another, and many accounts related to hiring make a point of emphasising this, but there are also many accounts of bigotry, which are sadly convincing. Patrick MacGill's account rings depressingly true. The first farmer he hired with raised the issue of religion even before they had left Strabane hiring fair.

> 'What's yer name? … A Papist? … All Donegals are Papists … That doesn't matter to me' … He went out [of the café] and left me with the servant. As he passed the window … [the servant] Mary put her thumb to her nose and spread her fingers out towards him. 'I hate Orangemen', she said to me; 'and that pig of a Bennet is wan of the worst of the breedin'.'[51]

Work in Scotland and England

> Oh, the far tawtie fields are calling me away,
> An' the stretchin' in the bothies on the straw,
> An' the old men moanin' at the breakin' of the day,
> An' the trekkin' when the mornin' in the raw…
>
> To the spirit-broken, quiet-spoken, tawtie-hokin' men,
> Rollin' out a prayer in Gaelic in the whiles,
> An' the Erris girls turnin' on the reekin' straw again,
> An' they dreamin' o' the magic o' the isles.[52]

Irish migrant workers were travelling to work in England as early as the medieval period. In the last two centuries, most labourers who went looking for seasonal work on farms in Britain were employed from mid-summer until late autumn, mainly with grain and vegetable cultivation – singling turnips, hoeing turnips, saving hay, harvesting grain, digging potatoes and gathering turnips and mangolds.

Tattie hokers

Large numbers of migrant workers from Achill Island in Mayo, and the Rosses and Gweedore in Donegal went to work in the Scottish potato harvest (Fig. 50). The numbers of these 'tattie hokers' increased greatly from the late

1840s, because of the desperation caused by the Great Famine, and the development of a national railway system during the 1850s, at the same time that Ayrshire and other areas in south-west Scotland were becoming important for the production of early potatoes.[53] As with other migrant workers, researchers have found it difficult to estimate overall numbers of potato harvesters, and official figures are almost certainly underestimates. A Scottish scholar, Heather Holmes, has calculated that in 1910 there were at least 2,000 Irish workers employed in the Scottish harvest, and this rose to a peak of more than 2,500 in 1918. A slow decline in numbers followed, with a faster decline after the Second World War. By 1971, only 600–800 Irish workers went to the Scottish harvest, and by the 1990s, numbers were negligible.[54]

Most of the migrants' work was provided by Scottish potato merchants. The merchants sometimes rented land from farmers on which they then planted potatoes, but usually they worked along with local farmers to produce a crop, or bought the potatoes as a crop in the fields at an agreed price per acre. The merchants employed 'gaffers', who were usually from the west of Ireland, to organise the harvest workers. The gaffer was responsible for recruiting a squad of harvesters (anything between 10 and 40 people), organising transport and accommodation, and supervising work in the fields. They could gain the respect of the workers, but in general they were thought of as 'hard men'.[55]

The Irish workers were generally thought to be quiet and hard working. In 1907, for example, the *Ayr Advertiser* commented that 'as a rule, they are capital workers and well-behaved'. This seems to have been due, in part, to the family connections between people in the squad. Before the 1960s, many squads were made up of members of extended families, including at least one older member, who supervised their behaviour.[56] The tattie hokers' good behaviour may also have been partly a consequence of their work. They were often too exhausted for energetic, or anti-social leisure activities.

Harvesting potatoes was the one type of seasonal farm work where significant numbers of Irish women were employed (Fig. 51). In 1907, it was estimated that around 70% of the Irish workers in Ayrshire were women, and this proportion grew until by the 1930s, the squads were said to be made up of women, girls and boys, and only a few adult men.[57] The conditions endured by potato harvesters in Scotland was the subject of intense discussion, and indeed scandal. The Donegal writer Patrick MacGill's brilliant autobiographical novel, *Children of the Dead End*, describes the misery endured by women workers in particular.

50 'Waling Potatoes, Renfrewshire' by William Marshall Brown (1868–1936). At least some of the women shown in this painting would have been from West Donegal or Achill Island in County Mayo. (Paisley Museum and Art Galleries, Acc. No.: A0207.)

51 Women tattie hokers. Numbers of women travelling to Britain as migrant workers rose sharply with the spread of railways in the late nineteenth century. Most of those travelling from West Donegal and Achill Island found work in the Scottish potato harvest, or as fish curers.

All day long, on their hands and knees, they dragged through the slush and rubble of the field. The baskets which they hauled after them were cased in clay to the depth of several inches and sometimes when emptied of potatoes the basket weighed two stone … Pools of water gathered in the hollow of the dress that covered the calves of their legs … Two little ruts, not at all unlike the furrows left by the coulter of a skidding plough, lay behind the women in the black earth. These were made by their knees.[58]

Workers were generally housed on or near the farm where they were working, and the accommodation provided could sometimes be disgracefully inadequate. Conditions were alleged to be especially bad in the south-west of Scotland. Harvesters usually began their season's work in the south-west because the harvest of 'Ayrshire' potatoes, known in this area as 'the green hoke', was some weeks earlier than in the north-east. In the south-western counties of Ayrshire, Galloway and Wigtownshire, farms were smaller than in the central lowlands and the big tillage areas on the east coast. Accommodation for harvest workers was relatively good on the big eastern farms, with purpose-built hostels sometimes provided, but on the small farms, conditions were a major cause of complaint. Patrick MacGill describes workers sleeping in filthy, rat-infested barns, with primitive washing and cooking facilities, and his account is backed up by many others. Not everyone agreed. An account by 'a Scottish farmer', published in 1905, the same period covered in MacGill's first novel, gave a much more positive account of these conditions, but when the glow of good intentions is removed, it tends to confirm the view that the accommodation was very bad indeed.

As regards sleeping accommodation, one hears from time to time of the hardships that Irish girls have to endure in Scotland in their work. But of late years there has been a great improvement in this respect … the accommodation that the farmer can provide is severely taxed for that short period, cow-sheds and other outhouses being used, but all are made as clean as it is possible in the circumstances to make them. The workers are not exposed to any cold, as while they are at these places it is the very height of summer. What appears to be the greatest hardship they have to endure is the absence of inside fireplaces at which in wet weather the workers may dry their clothes. The cooking is generally done outside at a large coal fire, and it seems to serve that purpose perfectly well, but when the girls come in from their work drenched with rain there is no way of drying the garments properly. This hardship, however, is one that farmers are at present endeavouring to relieve … I scarcely think that there is much room now for complaint.[59]

Tragedies at Kilnford farm and Kirkintilloch

Two horrific events focused attention on the conditions of potato harvesters. In September 1924, nine Scottish potato harvesters, five women and four men, died in a fire in their sleeping quarters above a granary at Kilnford farm in the Parish of Dundonald in Ayrshire.[60] In September 1937, the deaths of ten Mayo workers at Kirkintilloch in Dunbartonshire caused even more public concern. An account of the disaster was written by Anton McNulty in the *Mayo News* in 2007.

> The Kirkintilloch squad, including the gaffer, Patrick Duggan from the Points, Achill Sound, was made up of 14 females and 12 males with the majority coming from the townlands of Shraheens, Achill Sound, Saula and Dooagh. The majority of the squad had travelled to Scotland in early June and, after working on a number of farms from Ayrshire to the Lothians, travelled from Edinburgh and took up their residence at Kirkintilloch.
>
> The ten male workers were allocated a bothy, while the gaffer Patrick Duggan, his son Thomas and the remaining female workers slept in an adjoining cottage. Thomas Duggan, who was having difficulty sleeping because of a boil on his neck, raised the alarm at 1a.m. after he heard the crackling of the flames. He woke his father, Patrick Duggan, who in turn woke the female workers and escaped from the cottage. Despite desperate efforts, they were unable to open the door of the bothy. The Scottish foreman, John Mackie, who had the keys for the padlock, was awoken at 1.15a.m. but by the time he had got to the bothy and opened the door, it was engulfed in flames and the roof soon collapsed.
>
> Among the female workers were family members of the trapped men. Later in the night, many of them were found by local people in a hysterical condition and they were later treated for shock.
>
> The victims of the fire included three sets of brothers, John Mangan (17), Thomas Mangan (15) and Michael Mangan (13) from Pollagh,

John McLoughlin (23) and Martin McLoughlin (16) from Saula, Patrick Kilbane (14) and Thomas Kilbane (16) of The Points, Achill Sound. The remaining victims included Thomas Cattigan (19), Achill Sound, Owen Kilbane (16), Shraheens and Patrick McNeela (15), of Shraheens.[61]

Witnesses at the Inquiry held after the fire reported that the trapped men were heard shouting 'Oh dear! Oh dear!' Peadar O'Donnell has suggested that they were in fact shouting in Irish, 'A Dia! A Dia!' (Oh God! Oh God!).[62]

Pressure from some trade unionists and other concerned observers had led to some improvements in the accommodation provided for potato harvesters by the 1920s. The tragedies at Kilnford farm and Kirkintilloch increased pressure on local authorities to implement a series of bye-laws passed in the 1930s, which specified minimum safety and hygiene standards in accommodation. By the 1960s, conditions had noticeably improved. Bye-laws set under the Housing (Scotland) Act of 1966 led to the provision of hot water, electric light and gas or coal heating systems. The improvement continued into the 1970s, but by this time, the numbers of tattie hokers had declined greatly.[63]

Harvesting grain in England and Scotland

In 1905, M.G. Wallace distinguished between Donegal workers who travelled to Scotland and England for work in the grain harvest, and Connacht workers, who went to England.[64] Most of these Connacht men travelled singly or in groups of three or four. Like the spalpeens in Ireland, those travelling alone sometimes already knew of farmers in Britain who might employ them, either through contact made in earlier years, or through recommendations from neighbours or relatives. Those who went without making prior arrangements would tramp from farm to farm looking for work, or join with other workers they met in lodgings, or even on the road.

Hugh Paddy Óg Ward from Keadew in the Rosses, County Donegal, remembered whole families, including young children, closing up their houses and going away to work for the summer in the 1920s and 1930s. Hugh went to work in the Scottish grain harvest one year in the 1930s, after finishing a season working as a fish curer in Frazerburgh. He found work by going to a boarding house in Perth, which he knew was used by migrant workers. He met four older men from the Keadew, Arlans and Cruit areas of the Rosses who

52 A spalpeen with a sickle wrapped in straw rope (súgán). Irish harvest workers were known for their skill in reaping grain neatly, with little loss of either seed or straw.

were looking for a worker to make up a harvesting squad. Squads were commonly made up of four workers reaping with hooks or sickles (Fig. 52), and one person tying and stooking the newly-cut grain. Hugh was employed as a binder and stooker. The squad was paid by the acre, and aimed to cut two-and-a-half acres a day. In good weather, work would begin at 8a.m. and continue until 6p.m. or 7p.m., with a short break for food around noon.

Compared to the squads of tattie hokers, grain harvesters formed an elite among migrant workers. Their status was reflected in their pay and living conditions. Hugh Ward said that he could earn thirty shillings a day as a harvester, which was as much as some workers at the time earned in a week. Accommodation was often in a vacant house, described as 'the Irishman's bothy'. Many Scottish workers disliked the bothy system, as the workers had to keep the bothy clean, and cook and wash clothes. Living conditions were often squalid. However, like the tattie hokers, Irish reapers were known for their good behaviour. One assessment, made in 1750, described them as 'useful, faithful, good servants to the farmer', a view that was repeated during the nineteenth century.[65]

Hugh Ward, as well as working in the fields, was given housekeeping duties.

I used to be in maybe half an hour before them … And there was a butcher used to come to the farm twice a week and I would get a shilling each from them before I'd go down, the day the butcher was coming … and you want to see the dish of meat I would get … it was all steak. Well, that would keep us going for a couple of days … then he came another day a week. So you had, say four of the working days, you had steak.[66]

If harvesters failed to find work, however, they had to come home. Mick McHugh of Hornhead, County Donegal, described one such occasion in the 1920s.

I done three weeks on the road and I couldn't get a tap to do … I tried seven farmers and I couldn't get an hour with them. I finished up one Sunday evening and I'd nothing in front of me only to come home again. I still had a pound in my pocket … 'I'll not break into it', I said …. I couldn't walk on the water home … I was up at the head of the Holy Loch that Sunday evening … This man came up to me and [offered] … me a job … ten shillings a week … but I could stay in the house and all … And I was in for two weeks working with him and I got the loan of a bicycle … and I fell [off] and I broke my collarbone … I had to come home. And I got to Glasgow and the boat … A man told me to speak to Paddy McGuinness. He used to run the pub on the boat, and this man said, 'There he is. Go and speak to him.' … He said, 'Have you got five bob with you?' [and he took that.] … I landed in Dunfanaghy with seven shillings.[67]

As with other kinds of migrant work, numbers travelling to Britain for the grain harvest grew with the development of the railway system and steam ships. In the long term, however, mechanisation of harvesting and the uncertainty of finding work increased the attractiveness of other options. During the twentieth century, more people looked for permanent work in English and Scottish cities, and if they succeeded in finding a job, they were reluctant to leave it for farm work. By the end of the Second World War, permanent emigration had largely replaced seasonal movements, and for migrants and their families, Ireland increasingly became a place to visit for holidays. However, the number of English accents heard in West Mayo, and Scottish accents that are common in West Donegal, are a clear testimony to ongoing ties.

Working relationships between farmers and labourers

It is clear from the accounts given above that conflicts between migrant workers and the farmers who employed them could be very bitter. This was equally true for the weekly-paid day labourers who made up the vast bulk of agricultural workers. Many eighteenth- and nineteenth-century observers reported hostile relationships, and similar accounts can be found during the following century. Complaints of bad treatment were very common. Workers from west Limerick alleged that the east Limerick farmers who employed them would 'get the last stroke of work out of a boy', and one account relating to experiences in the 1860s described the way servants were treated as, 'Ní bheadh meas madra orthu.' (They wouldn't have got the respect given to a dog.)[68] However, it is important to emphasise that very warm, friendly relationships could develop between workers and their employers. Mary Carberry's account of her childhood beside Lough Gur in County Limerick, which also centred on the 1860s, describes well-ordered working arrangements presided over by her wise, kindly father. This farm employed both live-in and day labourers, and full-time and seasonal workers:

2 house-maids, who shared a bed-room in the farmhouse

A children's nurse/governess

4 cottiers

A head dairy woman

4 cottiers' wives who milked the farm's 50 cows, helped by their daughters

2(?) farm boys, who slept in a furnished room above an outbuilding

A head ploughman

A 'Head man' (farm manager)

A local smallholder, who was employed at harvest time to build hay and grain stacks

A spinning woman, who came just after sheep shearing, to spin the farm's fleeces.

Spalpeens, hired for potato digging.[69]

Even in this idyllic situation, however, status differences between the family and workers were clearly marked, as were differences between different categories of worker. The farm boys and ploughman ate in the farm kitchen, but at different times. Apart from mealtimes, the farm boys were only allowed into the farmhouse for daily prayers; the family and workers would say the Rosary together every day at 9p.m.[70]

Mary Carberry's account suggests that spalpeens, like the farm's other employees, fitted well into local working life.

> Spalpeens, coming usually from Kerry and Cork, were hired for the potato digging in October. My father's head man, Dick Dooley, used to go into Bruff on a Sunday in late September … and after Mass he inspected and hired the required number of spalpeens who were waiting in the street to be hired by the highest bidder. The same spalpeens came year after year to our farm; quiet and unobtrusive they were.[71]

Farm servants, who were in some ways the most vulnerable group of workers, especially if they were young and working for strangers, might also be lovingly cared for by their employers. Cormac McFadden from Roshin in north Donegal described several happy experiences he had as a teenager. He was hired during the period between 1908, when he was eight years old, and 1920. On one very small farm, his employers were his 'kin by marriage'.

> Oh, you wouldn't get [left] … to yourself for the neighbours and going out and in to the neighbours, … and they were all over at the table playing [cards]. I wasn't playing. I [would] … put on a big pot of praties [potatoes] and when I took them off, aw you could eat your fill of them … and you wouldn't call the king your uncle!

In 1919, at Dunfanaghy hiring fair, he met an elderly woman whom he had worked for some years before.

> She wanted to get me back … I came down the hill from Roshin and I met her … and [she] shook hands with me crying, and she says, 'You'll come back to me this rabble [hiring] fair.' 'Well', says I, 'No Cissie, I can't come back, for my father has me hired with this Willie Henderson of Murroe.' And she says, 'I'll give you as much as Willie Henderson is giving you and more if you'll come to me.' 'Well', says I, 'He's down in the town and you can talk with him … I have nothing to do with it.' And he wouldn't retract his word then, he wouldn't sell me, so I went to Hendersons.[72]

We have no way of quantifying the relative frequency of good or bad treatment, but as accounts of hiring such as Patrick MacGill's make clear, antagonism seems to have been an inbuilt part of many working relationships, with both farmers and workers viewing one another with suspicion and hostility. Tensions were also common between seasonal migrants and local residents. Some migrant workers were seen as easy prey for local thugs, or as anti-social incomers with no place in local society. One eighteenth-century Gaelic poem, by Uilleam Buí Mac Ghiolla Chiarán, makes the bad reputation of spalpeens clear.

> I thought you were a stranger from Co. Meath
> Who would steal my hat, my stick and my trousers;
> The spade from the door, the shovel and the pick
> The nice candle grisset and my little stump of a pipe.[73]

In terms of working relationships, the most intense hostility to spalpeens came not from respectable farmers, but from local labourers, who saw them as rivals, responsible for keeping wages low. Throughout the nineteenth century, threats and beatings endured by migrant workers were reported in counties Cavan, Leitrim, Limerick, Longford, Mayo, Meath and Tipperary. In the latter county, it was claimed that the incomers were sometimes mutilated and, on occasion, murdered.[74]

> One day the O'Sheas [of Ballynatten, County Tipperary] had two spalpeens digging the potatoes. While these boys were eating their dinner they left their spades in the garden and when they returned to the garden afterwards the two spades were labeled and on the labels there was a notice ordering them to leave before evening. The spalpeens took no notice and worked on until evening. When they had their supper eaten they sat around the fire. There were other visitors at the house also, a woman and a small child. While they were talking within, the house was set on fire and not one of them escaped. When people were clearing away the remains of the house afterwards, they found the child drowned in a churn of milk. She was probably put there for safety by the mother.[75]

This account was written down by a schoolchild in the 1930s, many years after the period in which the alleged atrocity was said to occur, and some caution is needed in assessing its accuracy. For example, it would be unusual for a churn full of milk to be sitting in a farm kitchen. However, it expresses the intensity of antagonism towards spalpeens which is also frequently reported in less dramatic accounts.

Organised labour

Trade union activists found special difficulties in organising farm workers, because of their mobility (especially in the case of migrant workers),[76] their isolation (there might be only one or two labourers on a farm) and also because of the very personal, face-to-face relationship many had with their employer.[77] Many labourers also found more satisfaction in carrying out the practicalities of their work than urban industrial workers. Oral testimonies sometimes claim that a labourer was more interested in ensuring good crops and impressive livestock on the farm than their employers. Despite this, and the attractions of living in a clean, relatively healthy environment, however, labourers suffered very poor working conditions. They were some of the poorest paid, downtrodden workers, and tensions between them and their employers could boil over into violence.

The level of violence in rural Ireland during the eighteenth and nineteenth centuries was commented on at length by contemporaries. Some of this would now be called 'recreational violence'. For example, some faction fights, which could involve thousands of combatants, had the same mix of motives as modern gang fights (Fig. 53). More serious motives underpinned millenarian movements such as the 'Rockites', which swept through Limerick, Kerry, Cork and Tipperary in 1822. The insurgents, who gave allegiance to a mysterious 'Captain Rock', had an amalgam of political, sectarian and economic goals, expressed through violence, myths and rituals.[78]

More everyday tensions could arise between farmers and labourers because of new technology and related changes to working arrangements. For example, in the first decades of the nineteenth century, the introduction of improved ploughs, which could be operated by one person rather than the three required to operate older 'common' ploughs, led to complaints of loss of employment.[79] The introduction of labour-saving reaping machines, mowing machines and threshing machines was unpopular with many labourers, and some were damaged by protestors. In 1858, for example, reaping machines on farms at Outrath and Thomastown in County Kilkenny were destroyed. Reaping

53 Women faction fighters. Faction fights were the most spectacular instances of recreational violence in nineteenth-century Ireland. Loosely structured groups such as the Shanavests and the Caravats would meet to fight by arrangement. Spontaneous fights, sometimes involving thousands of people, would also erupt at fairs.

machines were also smashed in Counties Waterford and Tipperary, and in the latter county a threshing machine was destroyed at Barron Court.[80]

Any labour-saving device could be seen as a threat to a labourer's livelihood. Scythes, for example, had been used for mowing hay on Anglo-Norman estate farms, but they only became common in the grain harvest during the nineteenth century. It has been estimated that grain can be cut four-to-five times faster with a scythe than with a sickle, the most common tool in earlier times.[81] Incidents of scythe smashing were reported from Kilkenny and Tipperary. These were attributed to spalpeens.[82]

The best-known labour dispute in farming, between Captain Boycott and workers on Lord Erne's estate at Lough Mask in 1880, gave the world the concept of the 'boycott', when the estate's labourers refused to harvest the landlord's grain. Fifty 'Orange labourers' eventually saved some of the harvest, but feelings were so bitter that Captain Boycott found it expedient to leave the area for a year (Fig. 54). Similar actions by workers on other estates, including

54 Captain Boycott leaving Ireland. In 1880, workers on Lord Erne's estate at Lough Mask refused to harvest the estate farm's grain. The struggle between the workers and the land agent Charles Cunningham Boycott was reported internationally. The grain was eventually harvested by Orangemen from South Ulster, working under armed guard, but the use of non-co-operation, the 'boycott', became a standard tactic of non-violent resistance worldwide.

one at Clonakilty in County Cork, where 1,000 acres of grain were at risk, led to the formation of an Orange Emergency Committee, which claimed to have helped boycotted landlords in nineteen counties.[83]

In the early twentieth century, trade union activists had some success in organising farm workers. Even migrant potato harvesters took some effective collective action, particularly in 1918, when they caused significant disruption to the Scottish potato harvest by refusing to go to Scotland until their demands were met. At least some of these were achieved, including a 50% to 100% increase in their wage rates and the right of women workers to have separate sleeping accommodation.[84] Even after this successful campaign, however, several reports claimed that many harvesters who benefitted from it had never even heard of a trade union.[85]

Fingal farm labourers' dispute, 1913

Many of the issues arising from attempts to organise farm labourers by trade unions can be seen in the dispute between farmers and labourers in Fingal, north County Dublin, in 1913, as documented by Eugene Coyle.[86]

At the time of the dispute, north Dublin had a large number of middle-class farmers and a number of large estates that dominated the production and distribution of food within Dublin city. In late spring 1913, the labour leader Jim Larkin toured north County Dublin trying to organise farm workers, in the face of opposition by local clergy and employers. Larkin believed that 'the harshness and misery of the agricultural labourer's lot greatly rivalled in intensity the very worst experiences of [their] inner city colleagues'.[87] Local branches of the Irish Transport and General Workers' Union (ITGWU) were set up to represent the interests of 'cottiers', farm labourers, shop workers and domestic servants. In April 1913, twenty farm workers walked off a farm near Drynanstown, but returned in a few days after the farmers who employed them threatened to evict them.

A bigger strike began in August 1913, when 608 unionised farm labourers walked off farms and estates in north Dublin in protest against the sacking and eviction of 'Larkinites'. At first, things went well for the strikers. A County Dublin Farmers' Association, formed in response to the action, negotiated with the union, agreeing a 20% increase in wages for male workers. However, in September, opposition to the strike became more effective. Larkin's great enemy, the press baron, businessman and politician, William Martin Murphy, urged farmers not to employ union members. Police reinforcements were drafted in to the area to protect farmers and non-striking workers, and hired Orangemen from Ulster were brought in to carry out essential work. The strike collapsed in mid-October, defeated, Coyle suggests, by worsening weather, hunger and evictions. Catholic clergy who opposed the strike stopped the distribution of food parcels from England, and Larkin had been imprisoned for sedition. By early November, most strikers were back at work on the employers' terms. Many of the strike organisers who were refused work either emigrated or joined the British army.

The north Dublin strike was one of a number of disputes, some of which led to attempts to organise on the part of both labourers and farmers. Several of these disputes were in County Cork. In Kanturk, for example, labourers went on strike for higher wages during the harvest of 1880. In June of that year the Irish Agricultural Labourers' Union was set up in Kanturk at a meeting organised by the Kanturk Labour Club and attended by around 2,000 people. Other local labourers' leagues and union branches were formed, but like the union organised in Kanturk, most did not last. Michael Davitt's Irish Democratic and Labour Federation, the Irish Land and Labour Association, and the Knights of the Plough were more successful, but all three organisations had also disappeared by 1900.[88]

It has been a central aim in Irish labour history to explain why Ireland never developed stronger labour organisations. What some socialists would still refer to as the 'objective conditions' which would lead to such developments – poverty, repressive legislation, social and political alienation, and committed activists – were all notoriously widespread in Ireland. Apart from the complex rural working relationships outlined above, part of the answer seems to be the commonly asserted one, that in Ireland, labour movements have often split over the national question. In Northern Ireland during the 1970s and 1980s, a number of fine initiatives attempted to put solidarity between workers at the core of their ideology, transcending all other relationships. Their efforts received an initial welcome from generous people attempting to go beyond murderous divisions, but sooner or later they would be asked to state a position on the national question. Attempts to set this on one side were received with suspicion, and any statement of aspiration, no matter how low-key, would split the movement. The importance of this fault line as far back as the 1880s can be seen in the involvement of the loyalist Orange Emergency Committee in breaking boycotts, and it also led to a split in the Irish Agricultural Labourers' Union formed at Kanturk, when the union included home rule for Ireland as one of its goals. The English Agricultural Labourers' Union split with the Irish union because of this, and the latter faded away, its leaders becoming involved in other activities.[89]

The demise of farm labourers

A minority of farm labourers achieved better living conditions in the later nineteenth and early twentieth centuries, especially with the provision of publicly funded labourers' housing. Negotiations for better wages were also sometimes successful, especially during crises such as the First World War, when minimum wages were agreed, and attempts were made to regulate working hours. In 1917, for example, an Agricultural Wages Board fixed a day's work as 10 hours in summer and 8–10 hours in winter. Wage rates were set at 20s.–25s. a week in summer, and 18s.–22s. 6d. in winter, the lower rates being set for the west of the country. However, even the Board recognised that implementing these terms of employment was extremely difficult, because of other aspects of working agreements.

Historians have debated whether Irish farm workers were becoming more like urban working-class people by the twentieth century. If labour activists experienced difficulties organising farm workers, state bureaucrats also found themselves unable to formulate or regulate detailed terms and conditions. As David Fitzpatrick has pointed out, when it came to agricultural wages 'the "ordinary labourer" of the statistician's dreams was a rare … creature'.[90] The different categories of farm worker and their related forms of payment were still entangled to an extent that it would have been a bureaucratic nightmare to categorise and quantify them in detail. In one attempt, the Board listed the 'customary benefits' received by some farm workers and set values on them. The figures in the table below are for County Donegal. Figures for eastern counties were higher.[91]

Maximum weekly values permitted by the Agricultural Wages Board (1917) for benefits and advantages provided by employers in lieu of payment in cash.

	s.	d.
Land, per statute acre		
a. Land, cultivated and tilled, per statute acre	0	4½
b. Land, cultivated, tilled, and manured, per statute acre	3	0
c. Land, cultivated, tilled, manured and seeded, per statute acre	4	0
Drills of potatoes to be measured and paid for at the same rates		
as a, b, or c above, according as the condition of a, b, or c apply	6	0
Potatoes (weekly rate of deduction per ton per annum)	1	6½
Fresh milk, per gallon	1	0
Grass of cow, grass only	1	11
Grass of calf till one year old	0	7
Keep of cow with grass and hay	3	10
Use of cow (a freshly calved cow for one year)	5	0
Grass of donkey	0	6
Grass of goat	0	3
Grass of sheep	0	6
Turf bank	0	6
Turf, cut, saved and carted, sufficient for workman for one year	1	9
Timber firing	1	0

(continued)	s.	d.
Board and lodging (seven days)	10	4
Board (seven days)	8	9
Board, per day	1	3
Dinner (seven days)	5	3
Supper (seven days)	1	9
Board and lodging, Males 18–21 (seven days)	10	0
Board and lodging, Males 16–18 (seven days)	7	0
Board and lodging, Females (seven days)	6	6

A note accompanying this table gave the value of a rented house, maintained by the farmer, as between 1s. and 1s. 6d. of the labourer's weekly wage.[92]

It is clear that farmers employing live-in farm servants, or cottiers, would be involved in ongoing, detailed documentation in trying to calculate such payments, and even then, when we consider the range of accommodation and food provided (anything from 'not fit for animals' to the same as the farmer's family), the usefulness of these figures as a guide to the monetary value of payments in kind is questionable. In 1922, the Department of Agriculture recognised the difficulties of trying to standardise working conditions in such detail, asserting that it was in fact dangerous for agricultural production to attempt to regulate labour on farms in ways that had 'no true relation to the realities of farming life [by] taking … ideas from factory life.'[93]

Agricultural labourers continued to be disadvantaged compared to urban workers, but perhaps the most striking thing about farm workers is their disappearance. The decline in numbers was seen as remarkable as early as the 1880s. In 1888, William Bence-Jones observed of County Cork, 'It is a most curious change. When I first began [in 1841] there were at least as many labourers as farmers, but they have nearly all gone away.'[94]

Official figures for labourers are probably underestimates, but the drop in their numbers was clear.

Number of rural labourers in Ireland

1841	1,100,000	1930	160,000
1881	350,000	1955	80,000[95]

Farm labourers had been the biggest sector in the work force in the mid-nineteenth century, but a hundred years later, their numbers were relatively insignificant. The Great Famine of the 1840s and its aftermath were major factors in starting the decline. Like nearly every famine, the Great Hunger hit the poorest people hardest, and farm labourers, more dependent on the potato than almost any other section of society, were desperately vulnerable. They died or emigrated in correspondingly huge numbers.

Farm labourers were also marginalised by changes in Irish farm production. From the mid-nineteenth century, a long-term, almost continuous swing from crop production to livestock farming was ongoing throughout Ireland. Before large-scale mechanisation, management of livestock required much less labour than arable farming. There was a decline in the number of farmers during the second half of the nineteenth century, but the decline in the numbers of farm workers was even greater. Between 1841 and 1911 the number of farmers declined by a quarter, while the number of farm workers declined by two-thirds,[96] and these trends continued throughout the twentieth century and beyond. In the new millennium the widespread use of contractors in crop production has meant less employment for farm workers, either temporary or permanent, than ever. Big dairy farms do often employ full-time workers, but in small numbers. As with the weakening of neighbourly ties, the disappearance of farm labourers has had a huge impact on the structure of farming society, and especially on the sense of community, which many rural people still treasure. In the following chapters, we will look at the notions people attach to the idea of community, to see what reality, if any, it represents.

Chapter 5

A sense of belonging

> Or is it that the unchristened heart of man
> Still hankers for the little friendly clan
> That lives as native as the lark or hare?[1]

THERE ARE TWO NOTIONS about life in the countryside that underlie the way many people look at Ireland's rural heritage; the idea of an unchanging 'traditional' way of life and, related to this, the idea of warm tightly-knit communities, where people looked after their family and neighbours, all of whom shared deeply ingrained, and unchanging, values (Fig. 56). The myth of Ireland as 'The Land that Time Forgot' was especially popular in tourist guidebooks of the mid-twentieth century, and a belief that there are places in rural Ireland where ancient ways still hold sway inspired folklife scholars like Estyn Evans, who carried out ground-breaking fieldwork throughout the country in the 1940s and 1950s.

> A significant factor in … the essential unity of Ireland … has been the retention, persisting in many areas into modern times, of certain attitudes towards the world and the otherworld … which had their origins in the Elder Faiths of pre-Christian times.

Evans believed that Irish rural life was deeply influenced by a 'neolithic substratum', which still profoundly influences cultural practices, attitudes and beliefs.[2]

Evans was not an Irish nationalist, but his approach to folklife was very much in tune with romantic nationalist models developed in Ireland and many other European countries since the mid-nineteenth century. Many early nationalist visions can now seem ludicrous, but they were initially a healthy reaction to much more negative views. As with any category of people in western society, country people, and rural society, have been stereotyped in both positive and negative ways. Since medieval times, many English, and some Irish colonial writers, have presented Irish country people (especially Catholics) either as drunken, treacherous and violent thugs, or as charming

55 'A Wall of Seaweed Sweating in the Sun' by Philip Flanagan, acrylic on linen (2012).

56 A rundale community at Machaire Clochair, Gaoth Dobhair, County Donegal. Social theorists define communities in different ways, for example, by the amount of face-to-face interaction between people, or by a sense of belonging. Using either of these criteria, rundale farming groups were communities. (Photo: Glass coll., courtesy Trustees, National Museums Northern Ireland.)

idiots, wayward children who had to be guided by their betters. In a positive reaction to this, some nineteenth-century nationalist writers, supported by folklorists and antiquarians, developed equally inaccurate stereotypes of Irish country people as noble (or picturesque) 'tradition bearers', living in timeless harmony with nature, and with one another.[3] The quest for a national essence was a driving force in many countries in Europe and elsewhere. In building up a model of their particular homeland, activists searched for a pure, unspoilt way of life, 'the real thing', in remote and beautiful areas, which had distinctive cultures. The west of Ireland fitted these criteria wonderfully well (Fig. 57).

> Oldest Ireland lives along the western seaboard of Donegal, in Connemara, Kerry, and Cork. It is Gaelic speaking and for that reason preserves the customs of the antique world. It is so different from the rest of Ireland that even the rest of Ireland hardly knows it … I write of a deeply buried substratum which only the most devoted and trained folklorists can, with patience … touch.[4]

57 Paul Henry, 'The Potato Diggers' (1911). The West of Ireland was opened up to travelers with the spread of railways in the nineteenth century. The painter Paul Henry was so overwhelmed by the beauty of Achill Island when he came from Paris on a visit that he tore up his return ticket and dedicated the rest of his life to painting the West.

Search for an essence: Irish Moiled and Kerry cattle

The search for the real (fíor Gaelach) thing was not only confined to Irish speakers. At its height a very wide range of artifacts, practices, and even plants and animals were scrutinised and sometimes accepted as elements of the national essence. For a brief period around the end of the nineteenth century, 'cultural nationalism' transcended class and ethnic divisions, and some Anglo-Irish gentry and Northern Unionists adopted aspects of Irish culture as markers of identity, seen as separate from party political associations. As in

58 A woman herding Kerry cattle at Slea Head. (Photo: Ó Muircheartaigh coll., Muckross Research Library.)

59 Dairy maids, dairy-hands and others in the farmyard of the Muckross estate. The Kerry bull is held by the head herdsman. (Info: Patricia O'Hare. Photo: Vincent coll., Muckross Research Library.)

Scotland and other European countries, manifestations of national culture were identified in landscapes, buildings, dress, music, food, and even breeds of dog. Farm livestock were also included. Kerry cattle were kept both as productive livestock and distinctively Irish ornamental features (Figs. 58 and 59). This was particularly the case in the south-west, where landed families who kept them included the Hilliard and Vincent families of Killarney and the Knight of Kerry. Elsewhere in Ireland, the Duke of Leinster had a herd at Carton near Maynooth, and an important herd of Kerry cattle was kept by the Robertson family as far north as Limavady on the rich lands east of Lough Foyle.[5] The Kerry, which had been known as 'the poor man's cow', became more closely associated with the gentry. In 1890, an RDS report commented that 'Mostly all the prizes [for Kerry cattle] go to gentlemen … the farmers of the Kerry mountains seem to take so little interest in cultivating this valuable breed.'[6] As the movement towards home rule grew after 1910, the attempt to develop harmlessly picturesque manifestations of Irish culture dwindled away, but the association of Kerry cattle with the landed gentry continued. In 1949, it was claimed that the Kerry had 'remained largely in the hands of well-to-do folk and … rarely is it found in commercial herds of ordinary farmers'.[7]

60 Irish Moiled cattle. The Irish breed with the most complex folklore, including claims that the cattle are mentioned in the Bible, that they were kept by the Vikings, and when their markings are right, that they are fairy women in disguise.

In some ways, the association between Irish Moiled cattle (Fig. 60) and the social classes who developed and managed the breed is the converse of the situation just described for Kerry cattle. Initiatives to develop a registered breed from local types of polled cattle were attempted by some gentry landowners in the Irish midlands during the late nineteenth century, but a breed society was eventually established in Northern Ireland in 1926.[8] This led to claims that Moiled cattle were 'Ulster's own cow', and at the start of the new millennium, the most enthusiastic breeders were northern middle-class farmers. Irish Moiled types of cattle appear in early Irish literature and their antiquity as a breed is also asserted in claims that the Vikings brought them to Ireland, and even that they are 'the oldest breed of cattle in the world', allegedly being mentioned in the Bible.[9]

However, while the folklore associated with both Kerry and Irish Moiled cattle does have ancient elements, the symbolic significance given to both breeds is best understood as a response to modern social and political change.

The notion that an ancient Irish culture can be found almost intact in remote areas still sometimes appears in major literature such as Brian Friel's *Dancing at Lughnasa*, and the view that folklife scholars can scrape away more recent cultural accretions to uncover ancient realities still sometimes appears in academic texts, such as A.T.Q. Stewart's *Shape of Irish History*.[10] For most of us, however, the search for ancient cultural essences creates a hall of mirrors. Ireland has an ancient and in many respects, a glorious culture, but this is an ever-changing product of diverse influences that can only be identified through critical historical study, or expressed in the greatest Irish art. The claims for ancient cultural roots are best seen as a part of longing for rooted stability in a fast-changing, uncertain world.

A positive model of rural life in the past is still important for people as diverse as some environmental activists, New Age enthusiasts, and many suburban people who hang prints of western landscapes by Paul Henry in their living rooms and still enjoy recordings of 'Ploughing the Rocks of Bawn', or 'Cutting the Corn in Creeslough'. At this popular level, many country people also have a very positive view of rural society in the recent past. A common view is that life in the past, although poor and hard, was warmer, friendlier, and slower paced than the present, which is cold and impersonal by comparison.[11] Some of the prose used in describing this lost world is wildly enthusiastic.

> The entire dependence was … on the elements … The seasons became friends, each one bearing a different bounty, each one a welcome caller for a different reason. And bound up in this elemental circus, people lived together. Nobody was any different from anyone else; the same winds blew warm or cold on each family. This led to a wonderful and human tangibility, a community, a neighbourliness, which had to find expression somehow or other. It did, in co-operation, in neighbourly interest, in the helping with harvests and the delivering of children.[12]

When historians refer to an account of life in the past as a myth, they generally mean that it is a fantasy which doesn't stand up to critical scrutiny, and anyone who knows rural Ireland knows that, unfortunately, social harmony can be as difficult to find there as anywhere. The tensions and conflicts we have looked at in this book show that in many ways the model of the past as an unchanging time of equality and social harmony is absurdly inaccurate. However, it also points to real elements in rural society which deserve to be valued and celebrated. The myth is not all false.

Do communities exist?

The idea of a past golden age just outlined, and the concept of local rural communities, became popular subjects for researchers and social activists in the early twentieth century, ironically so as Eric Hobsbawm has pointed out, 'Never was the word "community" used more indiscriminately and emptily than in the decades when communities in the sociological sense became hard to find in real life'.[13]

The changing notions of what makes a community have been well-summarised by Gerard Delanty, and we can place Irish discussions of the concept by outlining some of this overview.[14] He shows that communities can be seen positively – as providing security, a sense of belonging, something crucial to happiness – or negatively – as suffocating and potentially oppressive. The positive view seems to dominate, however, expressed as a sense of loss. The sociologist Max Weber and others believed this sense of loss dated back to the Middle Ages and the decline of the certainties of medieval society.

The idea of a community as based on values of tradition, a moral entity, as opposed to society, which was increasingly seen as an alien, objective entity, became prevalent in the twentieth century, when 'community' came to be seen either as an alternative to modernity or as the real basis of social integration. Ferdinand Tönnies (1887) was one of the first scholars to stress this perceived distinction between society and community. With modernity, society replaces community as the primary focus for social relations. Community is 'living', while society is mechanical. Community is rooted in locality and is 'natural', while society is more 'rational', and sustained by relations of exchange. For Delanty, however, the idea of community is, in the end, a modern myth.

> The modern world has … been marked by a penchant for the cosy world of community, belonging and solidarity where the individual could feel at home in an otherwise homeless and increasingly insecure world … Community is … an expression of the search for something destroyed by modernity, a quest for an irretrievable past which is irrecoverable because it may never have existed in the first place.[15]

The notion that rural life has been unchanging in Ireland is to ignore the struggle for ownership of land, and the massive and rapid changes in technology and related upheavals in working and domestic life that would be more accurately described as evidence of an ongoing revolution than timeless continuity. Lorna Sage, discussing life in the Welsh and English borders in the mid-twentieth century, described a situation that can also be seen in Ireland.

> Farming life seemed a perpetual-motion machine, or an effect of gravity, something cyclic and unstoppable. Actually, it was because this kind of small-scale tenant farming was vanishing that the impression of stubborn resistance was so strong. Ways of life have been dying out in rural England time out of mind, at least for two hundred and fifty years since the great wave of eighteenth-century enclosures. It's the sense of an ending that's timeless.[16]

During the twentieth century, a newer, negative view of rural society became widespread among many city dwellers. This view, far from celebrating rural harmony and wisdom, denounces modern country people as ruthless spoilers of the environment. At around the same time, and especially in the 1980s, it had become clear to anthropologists working in Ireland that 'communities' were no longer tenable as the object of ethnographic study, if they ever had been. They were increasingly regarded as social constructions based on out-dated structural-functional models.[17] S.L. Popkin, for example, accused academics who argued for the existence of such communities of 'romantic scholarship', an approach which ignored the conflicts and calculations of rural life.[18] Many modern sociologists have also questioned the usefulness of the term community, but as Delanty rightly says, if we reject it, we will have to replace it with another term.[19] Although the notions of ancient, traditional lifestyles and close communities can be labeled as myths, this does not mean that they are completely untrue or unimportant. As E.P. Thompson stressed when he was discussing the notion of the village community in England, 'To say that it was a "myth" is not to say that it was all false; rather it was a montage of memories, an average.'[20] Irish country people's notions of tradition and community are based on a selective view of the past that can be dismissed as inadequate, but they express deeply felt experiences.

'Man of Aran'

Positive and negative aspects of 'folk community' models can be seen in one of the most famous, and unashamedly romantic, portrayals of rural Irish life, Robert J. Flaherty's film of 1934, *Man of Aran* (Fig. 61). This has fundamental

61 Actress Maggie Dirrane collecting seaweed in the 1934 film, *Man of Aran*. Robert Flaherty's romantic film of life on the Aran islands has been subjected to ongoing scrutiny and deconstruction. Despite its inaccuracies, however, it conveys the scale of the struggle for survival in the face of almost overwhelming odds, the great achievement of thousands of Irish people during the last three centuries.

elements which we expect in such a creation, a sublime, tempest torn primeval landscape, in which a tightly-knit family of noble islanders battle to make a living on land and sea. As a major piece of 'ethnofiction' the film has been examined and deconstructed for decades, scholars pointing out, for example, that the shark fishing shown hadn't taken place for at least fifty years before the film was made, that no islander would have gone to sea in the conditions shown in the celebrated storm scene, that the farming scenes were filmed in an area which had never been cultivated, but had been chosen for its dramatic landscapes, that the islanders' clothing was deliberately archaic, and even that the rush candles used for lighting were a thing of the past by 1934.

John Messenger, an anthropologist who scrutinised the models of society and history used in the film, saw it as a product of both 'nativism' and 'primitivism', both of which he saw as distorting reality.[21] Messenger believed that primitivism idealised the past, and that, like nativism, its main function was to provide 'psychological compensation for frustrations created by personal and social disorganisation'. For primitivists, as for other romantics, folk culture was superior to modern culture; in folk society the family was the core social group, operating as a highly integrated, co-operative unit, individuals were content with their lives, and in general possessed character traits that 'civilisation' had perverted.

Realism is the great enemy of romanticism, but Messenger often sounded more like a disappointed romantic than a realist. Because Flaherty's vision wasn't all true, Messenger seems to have seen it as his own task to portray the Aran Islanders as indolent and vulgar, complaining of hardship while living off state benefits, and delighting in mass popular culture such as country and western music and demonstrations of brute strength.[22] His attack on the character of the Aran Islanders reads much more like a torrent of bad-tempered polemic, than a correction of 'the romantic fallacy'.

> [On Aran] dysfunctional cultural forms abound, as revealed, for example, in the prominence of inter-family, inter-village, and inter-island factionalism … The family is not a closely-knit, co-operative group, but is characterised by considerable antagonism between spouses, sibling rivalry, hatred of the father, and factionalism.

The 'normal' islander is presented as someone near psychological collapse.

> A high incidence of mental illness prevails … and the 'normal' personality betrays marked masochistic, hypochondriacal and depressive tendencies.[23]

This view of Aran is as distorted as those produced by excesses of nativism and primitivism. For anyone who has experienced the intelligence, generosity, dignity and sense of fun of so many Irish country people, claims that such invective is in some way 'scientific' seem at best a silly joke.

A sense of loss revisited

Placing community life and coherent tradition in the past invites contrasts to be made with the present. Modern cultural and social decay is accounted for in different ways. As we have seen in the discussion of the decline of neighbourly help, one reason given for the decline in tradition and community is the bad attitude of young people. For the artist Paul Henry, this was a sad reality on Achill Island in the 1920s, where he also saw evidence of cultural decay in the introduction of the horse-drawn plough!

I had always been attracted by the old people, the old age pensioners on the island … they represented a dying generation with a sturdiness of character and a dignity of manner which I noticed to my sorrow was passing. The younger people often lacked the graciousness of manner and the very decided instinct of good breeding so marked in their elders … I felt that I was watching the end of an epoch, the slow fading out of an era. I had seen the first furrow cut by the first plough that ever turned the soil of Keel. I was witnessing with sorrow the gradual discarding of the scarlet petticoat by the womenfolk.[24]

As with the myth of community, this view was not all false. In the 1960s, Hugh Brody described the alienation of young people in the west of Ireland. He recounted a conversation that he had in Connemara with a farmer whom he was helping in a hayfield. 'I told him that I enjoyed [the work] … He told me that his sons, two of whom were in the house, refused to do the work. "They won't do anything that's not machines and tractors and cars … They're right. They are too clever for this sort of thing."' Brody found that young women in particular were leaving 'Inishkillane'.

> The bond between the young women of the parish, and the traditional life has snapped almost completely. I have often seen a girl giggle as her father left the kitchen, as if there was something a little absurd in his demeanour … because the father represents the traditional milieu, he is a bit 'old-fashioned' and therefore, in the terms of a modern girl, a bit peculiar.[25]

Brody has identified a rejection of old ways of life and attitudes that does seem to become very widespread in rural Ireland during the twentieth century. As early as the first years of the twentieth century, many farm women were alleged to 'look down' on farming.[26] In our own experience many young men as well as women did not seem to value the older culture. This was well illustrated by the remark of a young Tory islander in the 1970s. He asked a group of students if they were going to a dance that night. 'It's a real dance, not a céilí.'

Most accounts of this sort of attitude are implicitly critical of the young people involved, but for many of them, urban life represented the possibility of freedom and happiness. This is well expressed by one of Edna O'Brien's heroines, reflecting on her first night in Dublin (Fig. 62).

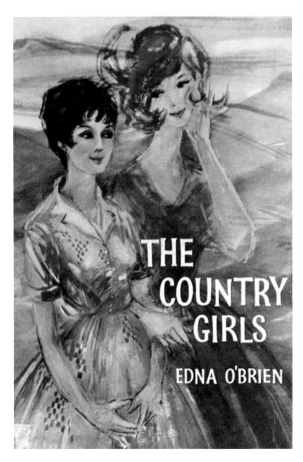

62 A detail from the cover of Edna O'Brien's novel *The Country Girls* (1960). Since the Great Famine of the 1840s, women have left the land in much greater numbers than men, and observers in the twentieth century are consistent in their claims that many of those who have stayed show little commitment to what are seen as traditional values.

> I knew that this was the place I wanted to be. Forever I would be restless for crowds and lights and noise. I had gone from the sad noises, the lonely rain pelting on the galvanized roof of the chicken house; the moans of a cow in the night, when her calf was being born under a tree.
> 'Are we going dancing?' Baba asked.[27]

This rejection can be seen as the negative version of a sense of loss expressed by many older country people; a sense that something basic is lacking in modern rural life. To a large extent this loss can be understood as a direct result of depopulation, but as we have seen, people also regret the tight cohesion of the farming family, and the lack of contact with their neighbours. To dismiss this as nostalgia, and scholarly attempts to describe it as 'romantic', is no more satisfactory than the blanket use of 'bourgeois' by some socialists.

The human warmth of Irish rural society, its cultural riches of language and music, and the ingenuity of its farmers in overcoming poverty and injustice are vital, and sometimes ancient realities. The farming year and the turning of the seasons have been a powerful metaphor for security and harmony since earliest history.

> While the earth remaineth, seedtime and harvest, and cold and heat, and summer and winter, and day and night shall not cease.[28]

Farming directly links the natural cycle with social relationships in ways that can give us a deep sense of belonging, a sense of coming home.

> And though to keep my brain and body alive,
> I need the honey of the city hive,
> I also need for nurture of the heart,
> The rowan berries and the painted cart,
> The bell at noon, the scythesman in the corn,
> The cross of rushes, and the fairy thorn.[29]

In the following chapters we will examine ways this heritage has been investigated and celebrated in rural exhibitions and events, beginning with the most basic tillage operation – ploughing. One of the key points emphasised will be the ways in which events such as horse ploughing matches, initially promoted to encourage modernity, have come to represent a lost or threatened way of life, acting as a symbol of community and belonging.

63 'St Brigid's Day Ploughing' by Philip Flanagan, oil on paper (2002).

Chapter 6

Horse ploughing matches: history and heritage

In many respects the history of the plough in Ireland is the history of the country and local societies have made their own unique contribution to the art of competitive ploughing. What finer sight indeed, is there than a field of straight furrows![1]

Origins

Ploughing is often regarded as the basis of agricultural production, a view aptly summed up by County Down veteran horse ploughman and farmer Bertie Hanna (Fig. 64) who said 'if you don't plough you don't sow, and you've no crop'.[2]

Although horses were regarded by improvers as the primary draught animal for ploughing, there were also classes for mules, bulls, oxen and heifers at early nineteenth-century ploughing matches.[3] During the nineteenth century, agriculturalists and observers considered Irish agricultural practices as backward and unsystematic (Fig. 65). The agricultural societies of the period saw ploughing matches as a means of addressing the 'problem' and encouraging new farming techniques by promoting the use of improved plough types and tillage practices through competition.

In 1813 the Farming Society of Ireland argued:

> If gentlemen in the country, would by little premiums or by ploughing matches or by other means facilitate the introduction of good ploughs amongst their tenantry or neighbours, agriculture would be advanced, and prejudice so deplorably prevalent, would be gradually done away with.[4]

A 'constant reader', writing to the *Irish Farmers' Gazette* in 1846 on the subject of ploughing matches, remarked:

64 Bertie Hanna (on left) competing at the Ulster Folk and Transport Museum's horse ploughing match in February 2009.

> You corroborate an opinion which I have for a long time entertained by attaching so much importance to 'ploughing matches as a means through which we may yet expect to see great and extensive improvements realised'. To no object better calculated to promote the interest of the Irish Farmers or secure their adhesion to an agricultural society could its members direct attention with so much advantage.[5]

In Ireland, agricultural societies were organised on a local and national basis and were mainly patronised by the landed gentry. The activities promoted by the agricultural societies, such as ploughing matches, were perceived, by those involved landlords, not only as a means for encouraging what they considered

65 Anti-Irish caricature, lampooning the practice of ploughing by the tail. E. Dubois, *My Pocket Book; or Hints for 'A Ryghte Merrie and Conceited' Tour in Ireland* (London, 1808), p. 82.

improved agricultural methods among their tenantry, but also as a means for fostering class alliances between landlords and tenants. For example, in 1817, the Marquis of Downshire, patron of the Hillsborough Farming Society, County Down, when distributing the prizes at the society's ploughing match, proclaimed that among his reasons for giving out premiums 'was to promote the spirit of emulation amongst his tenantry'. He further observed that he always considered 'the tenant as the steward of the landlord's property – and as such entitled to his fostering protection – their duties were reciprocal, and their interests should be for ever united'.[6]

Although hailed as a relationship of mutual interest, the landlord–tenant alliance promoted by improving landlords was, at its best, a class based paternalism primarily designed to maintain the status quo and the interests of the landed gentry. In the early nineteenth century the most prominent agricultural society promoting 'district' ploughing matches to improve tillage practices was the Farming Society of Ireland. Established in 1800 under 'the auspices of the chief nobility and gentry of Ireland' it was said to have:

> … the full concurrence of and patronage of the government, and the specious advantage of parliamentary aid; which patronage and assistance were considered as a boon to the landed interests.[7]

To protect 'landed interests', the society's applications for premiums for 'district' ploughing matches were restricted to landed gentry who were members of the society and involved in organising the district match. The society's notice for proposals for district ploughing matches in spring 1818 stipulated:

> GOOD PLOUGHING being essential to improved husbandry, the Society will continue Premiums to encourage Ploughing Matches next Spring, in different Districts of Ireland, the particulars of which will be published with the next Spring Premiums; and in order to enable the Directors to determine on the situation where such District Ploughing matches will be … such noblemen or gentlemen as are desirous of availing themselves of these Premiums, are required to give notice to the Secretary, before the 1st of January, 1818, after which day no proposal for a District Ploughing match will be received.[8]

The main socio-economic group within the farming community that the society wanted to encourage to use improved farming methods was those of 'better means', often referred to as strong farmers, from the 'middling to lower classes', and of a 'sober and industrious character'.[9] This was reinforced through the society's, strictly vetted, annual scheme for the sale of improved ploughs from its implement factory at reduced prices.[10] In order to purchase the ploughs, farmers were required to produce the following certificate endorsed by a clergyman of the parish in which they resided and a member of the society, to prove they were of good character and from a suitable social and economic bracket:

We, the undersigned, do hereby certify that

Of   in the County of

is a sober and industrious Farmer, living by husbandry, and possessed of a pair of Horses, Bullocks or Heifers, able to draw one of the before mentioned Ploughs, and we are of opinion that he will make a proper use of the same.

Signed

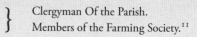
} Clergyman Of the Parish.
Members of the Farming Society.[11]

Premiums given at district ploughing matches were generally in the form of trophies, cash prizes or improved ploughs and were usually awarded to two distinct classes of competitors. Type one (see table below) were the landed gentry, who owned the plough but had ploughmen competing on their behalf. The person operating the plough was referred to as 'holding the plough'. Type two (see table below) were farmers who competed with an improved plough that was owned by them and 'held' by them or their sons. The term 'holding the plough' is still used at horse ploughing matches and its significance is discussed later. The society saw 'the spirit of emulation' as a strong motivating factor in advancing the cause of improvement.[12] As pointed out in other chapters of the book emulation has been a key element of family farming life in Ireland with farming knowledge and skills being passed from father to son and down the generations. By opening the Farmers Class to fathers and sons at district ploughing matches, the society was tapping into the farming family, the basic unit of Irish agricultural production, in the hope it would ensure the use of improved tillage techniques by future generations of farmers, ensuring that the 'bonds of society are knit together in harmony and prosperity'.[13]

The class nature of district ploughing matches was particularly glaring at the Kilkenny District Ploughing Match held on the estate of Sir Wheeler Cuffe, Bart, on 3 March 1817. Plots allotted for ploughing were divided into two classes with plots in Class I for the ploughs owned by the nobility and gentlemen farmers, and Class II for farmers or their sons holding their own plough. The *Irish Farmers' Journal and Weekly Intelligencer* recorded the entries for the ploughing match as follows:

CLASS I.	CLASS II.
The owners of ploughs, etc.	Farmers or their sons, holding their own ploughs.
1 The Right Hon. The Earl of Carrick.	13 James Byrne, Oldtown.
2 James Harris, Esq. Bennett's Bridge.	14 Luke Lanigan, Danville.
3 Abraham Prim, Esq. Ennisnagg.	15 Patrick Kelly, Archerslease.
4 Robert Flood, Esq. Farmley.	16 Edmund Brennan, Ballybur.
5 Edward Cullen, Esq. Castlecomer.	17 Patrick McAvoy, Castle Inch.
6 John Cahill, Esq. Sandford's Court.	18 Patrick Mackey, Newtown.
7 Hon. Col. Butler, Dunmore.	19 Patrick Knight, Burntchurch.
8 John Nowlan, Esq. Kilkenny.	20 John Ford, Burntchurch.
9 The Countess of Ormonde.	21 Richard Meany, Brownstown.
10 Timothy Nowlan, Esq. John's Well.	22 James Coor, Bawn Lusk.
11 Major Keating, C.B. Tenny Park.	23 Patrick O'Hara, Springhill.
12 John Prim, Esq. Kilree.	24 Thomas Martin, Newtown.
	25 Henry Neale, Walton-Hill.
	26 John Nowlan, Dunmore.[14]

Despite the class nature of the horse ploughing matches organised by the Farming Society of Ireland and the premium scheme for the purchase of improved ploughs being restricted to 'sober and industrous farmers' of 'better means', crowds of spectators from all strata of society flocked to the matches. In 1820, at the first ploughing match to take place in the Edenderry Farming District, a crowd of 'upwards of four thousand of the neighbouring gentlemen and peasantry' attended the match with 'lively interest – generally and eagerly displayed among all ranks, for the promotion of its objects'.[15] Such was the enthusiasm of the crowd at the 1817 Kilkenny District Ploughing Match, that the start of the match was impeded 'by the pressure of the multitude, whose eager desire to witness the performance could not immediately be restrained'. It was only after an hour's exertions by 'gentlemen on horseback' that the 'good sense of the people' prevailed and the ploughing could continue unimpeded.[16] However, despite the restoration of order, the fervent mood of the spectators remained unabated at the end of the match, when it was noted that the keen rivalry between competitors had 'imparted itself to the surrounding thousands, who shewed the most anxious interest in the decision'.[17] Passionate parish support for their ploughmen has been a constant factor in horse ploughing matches and a key element in their success and continuing survival.

Central to the basic rules for ploughing at matches developed by the Farming Society of Ireland were a demarcated style, a demarcated time, and a demarcated plot of land. For example, the style required for the Kilkenny District Ploughing Match to make a seedbed for oats was produced by ploughing a 'sod' the depth of 'five inches – breadth, eight' and 'that they be so cut that each part of the sod be a perfect parallelogram, that they lap over so as each succeeding sod shall cover three inches of the preceding one, by which means there will be an equilateral triangle of earth, each side five inches, to cover the seed which will fall into the grooves'.[18] In more recent times the 'parallelogram sod' has been referred to as the furrow slice and a style known as 'rectangular', which was one of several ploughing styles recognised by authorities in the early 1900s (Fig. 66). At a ploughing match near Dublin on 27 March 1817, the allocated time for ploughing with horses or mules was two hours and with bulls, oxen or heifers two-and-a-half hours, the demarcated size of the plot for both classes half a rood of ground.[19] The same basic elements of a demarcated style, a demarcated time and a demarcated plot of land have remained central to the rules of ploughing until the present day.

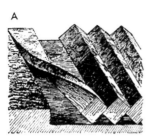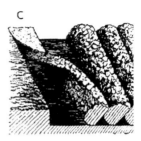

66 (a) rectangular work, (b) high cut work, (c) broken work, taken from R.P. Wright (ed.), *Standard Cyclopaedia of Modern Agriculture and Rural Economy*, vol. 9 (London, 1908), p. 252.

Given the unequal and potentially fractious nature of the landlord–tenant relationship, one explanation why ploughing matches appealed to both was that they shared the characteristic of what the anthropologist Victor Turner has termed 'dominant symbols', in that they could condense meanings and were seen as having many meanings, not all of them compatible with one another.[20] From this point of view, the ploughing field and the plots within it become demarcated spaces where ideologies are played out through the act of competitive ploughing. Horse ploughing matches differed from other kinds of sport of the period in that they were based on an activity central to the working and economic life of the participants and not a leisure pursuit. Ploughing matches, although viewed from very different vantage points, were a shared experience between landlord and tenant.

God on our side

> Turn up the brown, O man who ploughs!
> The waken'd earth to warming sun,
> And give all men their daily bread,
> Your work is God's for He has said
> He'll bless your work, and your plough – team too,
> Reward is sure for what you do.
> Then, Oh! Hurrah, sons of the soil,
> God speed the plough, God bless your toil.[21]

The evocation of a higher deity to oversee the crucial stages of agricultural production, such as ploughing, was a common practice in nineteenth-century

67 Logo from vol. 5, *Irish Farmers' Journal* (Dublin, 1817). The plough depicted in the logo is based on the improved Scottish swing plough, designed by James Small.

rural Ireland. This is reflected in the logo (Fig. 67) of the early nineteenth-century agricultural newspaper, the *Irish Farmers' Journal*. The logo is an illustration of what was held up to be the ultimate ploughing technology of the time. This was an improved Scottish swing plough pulled by two horses and operated by a single ploughman.[22] Ironically, despite the plough being promoted as a product of rational scientific principles, the refrain 'God speed the plough', calls upon the ultimate spiritual and moral authority to ensure the ploughing and ensuing crop is successful.

Unfortunately, in Ireland, due to religious divisions, one man's God is sometimes another man's anti-Christ. Irish landlords were predominantly Protestant ascendancy, many of whom were absentee landlords charging tenant farmers excessive rents. Most Irish landlords also saw themselves as part of a British colonial system presided over by the monarchy and ultimately God. Their God's administrator on earth was the Established Church, which was notorious for exacting extortionate tithes from a predominately Catholic peasantry. Consequently, any claims of 'fostering protection' from landlords or calls for reciprocal relationships of mutual interest would have fallen on sceptical if not hostile ears.

The situation of the close relationship between the interests of the dominant power and its related church was to be reversed in Ireland in 1937 with the adoption of the nation's second constitution, Bunreacht na hÉireann, which recognised the 'special position' of the Catholic Church in the state 'as the guardian of the faith professed by the majority of its citizens'.[23] This close relationship between church and state was to express itself at opening ceremonies of the National Ploughing Championships with the symbolic 'blessing of the field' by the Catholic bishop of the diocese, or his representative, in which the championship was held. One of the more dramatic blessings in the early years of the National Ploughing Championships took place on the eve of the outbreak of the Second World War. The championship was held on 8 February 1939 in Killarney, County Kerry, on the estate of the Earl of Kenmare, when an estimated crowd of 12,000 turned up, making it the best attended National Ploughing Championship to date. Eighteen counties competed with nearly 150 horses lent by Kerry farmers for the various events.[24] The blessing took place before the competition and the *Irish Times* describing the event noted:

> The day started with a procession of horses and ploughmen through the streets of the town on their way to the field, about half-way between the town and the lake shore, and at the park they were met by the Most Revd Dr O'Brien, bishop of Kerry, who gave them his blessing.[25]

In recent times a much more ecumenical view has been expressed at the National Ploughing Championships with representatives from Catholic and Protestant denominations sharing a stand in the field with the 'combined Churches Together effort … offering sustenance for body and soul, with shelter and cups of tea during the very wet and cold periods, and a quiet space for prayer and reflection'.[26]

Horse ploughing matches as an expression of community and the nation

During the late nineteenth and early twentieth centuries, with the passing of the Land Acts and compulsory purchase, ownership of the land in Ireland passed from the landlords to the tenant farmers. This did away with the need for class alliances between farmers and the landed gentry, and ploughing matches organised by farmers and local societies became widespread. At the same time standardisation and centralised control of farming activities also gathered momentum.[27]

Diarmuid Ó Giolláin argues that 'the tension between centre and periphery between centralism and localism, between hierarchy and grass roots can never be fully resolved and is part of the dynamics by which institutions change'.[28] Tension heightens with crisis and it was during the depression of the 1930s and the Economic War with Britain, when Irish agricultural production was under threat, that ploughing matches underwent dramatic organisational change. Keenly fought local parish and county matches (Fig. 68) became part

68 The well-known champion ploughmen Jeremiah, John and Dennis O'Sullivan displaying the three cups they won in Co. Cork, February 1925.

of a wider system of inter-county, national and international competitions that were significant factors in developing closer, if sometimes fraught, relationships between the state and the farming community.

The brainchild of progressive farmer and civil engineer, J.J. Bergin, from Athy, County Kildare, and farmer Denis Allen, from Gorey, County Wexford, the notion of an inter-county ploughing competition arose from a debate between the two, over which county had the best ploughmen. However, against the background of a depressed agricultural sector with a drastic decline in tillage and the widespread belief that 'the plough was Ireland's only redemption', it was decided to open the competition to other counties. A committee was formed and rules, classes and conditions of entry decided. The fledgling National Ploughing Association deliberated long and hard on its objectives, eventually formulating its enduring mission statement 'to bring the message of good ploughing to all parts of the country and to provide farmers with a pleasant, friendly and appropriate place to meet and do business'.[29]

In 1931, the first Inter-County Ploughing Contest was held on the land of Mr W.K. Hosie at Coursetown, County Kildare, on Monday, 16 February. In total nine counties took part in the Inter-County Ploughing Contest with forty-six ploughs on the field and an estimated 4,000 spectators turning up on the day. The classes and awards were as follows:

> Inter-County Class 1st, Wexford Team – Martin Conroy, Micheal Redmond, Edward Jones, all with Pierce ploughs; 2nd, Wicklow

Team – John Sulton, Christopher Roche and Cecil Fox; 3rd, Kilkenny Team – John Walsh, sen. (Sellar), John Walsh, jun. (Sellar), George Shirley (Ransome).

The other teams in order of merit were: 4th, Leix – Ed. Carroll (Ransome), Thomas Bambrick (Pierce), Patrick Butler (Ransome); 5th, Dublin – James Callaghan (Ransome), John Dowling and – Callan; 6th, Carlow – James Delaney (Ransome), M. Dowling (Pierce), James Harmon (Ransomes); 7th, Kildare – Wm. Ross (Pierce), James Wilkie (Ransome), Chris Leigh (Ransome); 8th, Offaly – Thomas Bracken, Laurence Bracken, James Meleady, all with Howards; 9th, Cork – Patrick and Michael Hawkes (Sellar), P.J. O'Donohoe.

Local Class – 1st, Chris. Carolan (Ransome), owner; John Melrose Leviston. 2nd, Patrick Kinsella (Ransome), owner; J. Yates, Leinster Lodge, Athy. 3rd, James Ryan (Ransome), owner; Joseph Fennelly, Quarry Farm, Athy. 4th, M. Fingleton (Ransome), owner; Thomas Yates, Grangemellon.[30] [The names in brackets after competitors names refer to the make of plough used by the competitor.]

A key feature of the competition which signalled to the farming community the determination of the organising committee to make it a permanent event was the awarding of individual and team trophies to be competed for on an annual basis. These were the ESMA (Estate Management and Supply Association) Perpetual Cup for the Senior Individual Ploughing Champion of Ireland and the David Frame Perpetual Cup for the Team Championship of Ireland.[31]

To insure that the event appealed to all age groups and the skill of horse ploughing was passed on to younger generations, young and novice ploughmen were included in the Local Class. The focus on young and novice ploughmen resulted in special praise for the 'excellent work' of third-placed James Ryan. Described as 'a boy of about 14 years of age', he was reported as having 'skilfully handled the Ransome plough belonging to Mr Joseph Fennelly, Athy'. Although there was a small tractor section and demonstration at the competition there was no official tractor ploughing class in the National Ploughing Championships until 1942. To reinforce the national status of the championships and standardise the type of horse ploughing executed, a style known as the 'National Style' was adopted. Another element of the Inter-County Ploughing Contest, which reinforced national identity and promoted

69 £1 bank note depicting a ploughman.

local commercial interests related to agriculture, was 'a special prize for the best work done by an Irish plough'.[32]

The anthropologist Turner saw the use of 'demarcated time and space' for a specific event involving 'staging and presentation' as ritual.[33] Drawing on Turner, A. Cohen argues:

> … ritual confirms and strengthens social identity and peoples' sense of location: it is an important means through which people experience community.[34]

During the 1930s and 1940s the National Ploughing Championship was to grow rapidly in size and, more importantly, become an event of huge national significance which was central to the government's propaganda campaign to bond the farming community and the state in the common purpose of making Ireland self-sufficient in food production. The acreage under grain and root crops had fallen by over forty per cent between the Great Famine and the outbreak of the First World War. The government of the early thirties believed that the only way to relieve a depressed agricultural sector, dependent on imported foodstuffs, and create self-sufficiency in food, was to institute a sustained tillage campaign. The notion of 'Irish bread, made from Irish wheat and ground in an Irish-owned mill' was to become 'a potent symbol of self-sufficiency.[35] The implementation of a propaganda campaign to encourage farmers to increase their acreage under wheat began in earnest with the onset of the Economic War in 1932. In retaliation to excessive tariffs placed on Irish agricultural exports, particularly the livestock trade, the government placed restrictions on the imports of wheat and other agricultural produce from Britain. In an effort to change agricultural production based on pastoral farming to one based on tillage, the newly appointed Minister for Agriculture, Dr James Ryan, appealed to patriotism rather than profit in his early propaganda campaign to make Ireland free of foreign wheat.[36] The embodiment of the farmer as a ploughman by the state occurred some years earlier, when he was depicted on the Irish pound note from 1929, 'back hunched, tilling the soil with his horses beneath a beaming sun' (Fig. 69).[37] Keenly aware of the value of propaganda in promoting the governments tillage policy, Ryan saw the National Ploughing Championship as an ideal stage for the state to engage with farmers on the issue of growing more wheat, and for farmers to hone their ploughing skills through competition. Most importantly for the Minister of Agriculture's campaign, it was an occasion for farmers and government to symbolically unite in a common purpose to save the nation.

Minister Ryan didn't waste time in implementing government policy. The Department of Agriculture, in an effort to encourage ploughmen to attend the 1933 National Ploughing Championship, gave county agricultural committees permission to give financial grants to local ploughing societies who entered teams.[38] To highlight that the Economic War was regarded as a serious threat to the state, and that farmers and the tillage campaign were central to the nation's survival, the National Ploughing Championship held on the 15 February at Newlands, Clondalkin, County Dublin, was raised to the level of a state occasion by the attendance of President de Valera and a retinue of state dignitaries. Upon their arrival due protocol was observed and they were received by members of the Joint Committee of the National Ploughing Association, including Chairman, Mr Richard Blake; Secretary, Mr J.J. Bergin, Hon. Secretary, Mr T. Ward, and Chairman of Dublin City Council, Mr John Shell.[39]

No opportunity was missed by senior state representatives to mingle with competitors and express a keen interest in the work of the ploughmen. The *Irish Times* reported:

President de Valera, with Dr Ryan, Minister for Agriculture, and Mr Aiken, Minister for Defence, were present during a great part of the day and displayed keen interest in the work of the various competitors. Others amongst the large gathering present were Senator O'Hanlon, Mr P. Belton, TD; Professor Drew, Dean of the Faculty of Agriculture, University College, Dublin.[40]

The symbolic bonding of ploughmen and state continued in the evening at the 'largely attended' championship dinner, with mutual praise from the speakers on the help given by the Department of Agriculture and the quality of the work executed by the ploughmen, with promises of better times ahead for the farmer. The *Irish Times* noted:

> In proposing the toast of 'Prosperity to Ireland', the Chairman [Mr Richard Blake] thanked all who had helped to make a success of one of the best ploughing matches held in the country. They could not have done so well were it not for the whole-hearted support which they had received from the Department of Agriculture, backed by their zealous Minister for Agriculture …

> Dr Ryan, Minister for Agriculture, replying, said that the toast of prosperity to Ireland could not be proposed on a more fitting occasion … He was delighted to see that the men behind the plough were taking an interest and pride in their work. It was up to the County Committees of Agriculture and to the government to try to give the farmer a better living in the future.[41]

In Northern Ireland in the 1930s, ploughing matches were contested at local level until 1937 when the governing body of ploughing, the Northern Ireland Ploughing Association, was formed at a meeting in Belfast between the Ulster Farmers' Union and representatives from over thirty local ploughing societies. The Ulster Farmers' Union still exists and still represents the interests of farmers up to government level. Also still in existence and affiliated to the Ulster Farmers' Union is the Northern Ireland Ploughing Association, whose principal function is to set the rules for competition and organise an annual ploughing match.[42]

From the outset the NIPA annual ploughing match had an international dimension and was used as a means to symbolically bond the state and the

70 Lone competitor from the Isle of Man sporting the Manx flag at the first International Ploughing Championships in Northern Ireland, February 1938.

farming community and define its boundaries through competition. Nailing its colours to the mast the main aim of the association, as laid out in the conditions of membership, was 'the maintenance of a high standard in the ancient and vital art of ploughing … and friendship amongst ploughmen in the British Isles and further afield'.[43] The first International Ploughing Competition, held on the farm of J.C. Drennan, Carse Hall, Limavady, County Derry, on 14 February 1939, had over 20,000 people attending and 107 competitors taking part. Ploughmen from the British Isles included 9 from Scotland, 5 from England, and those from 'further afield', eleven from the Irish Free State and one from the Isle of Man (Fig. 70).[44] The *Belfast Newsletter*, describing the occasion colourfully, highlighted regional differences between competitors and, with a slight hint of pathos, the carnival atmosphere of the sideshows:

> The competitors brought their own ploughs, of the 'chill' [wheel] and 'swing' [wheelless] varieties. The horses were all supplied by local owners, and one may reasonably suppose that the County Derry horses

found it difficult to understand the words of command voiced in accents from places so far apart as Aberdeen, Warwickshire and Wicklow … The horses were gaily bedecked with red, white and blue ribbons and even flowers.

Nearby a 'wheel of fortune' operator, inveigled the countryman to try his luck, a religious mission meeting made an effort to save sinners and from time to time a loudspeaker 'broadcast' Irish jigs and folk songs.[45]

Although local horse ploughing matches continued during the Second World War, the Northern Ireland International Match was suspended for the duration of the war. Meanwhile, 'south of the border', the promised 'better living in the future' for farmers came in the shape of a wheat bounty. With this added incentive, the acreage under wheat during the 1930s steadily grew to 255,000 acres in 1939, twelve times the amount grown in 1932.[46]

Although it had grown significantly, and the acreage under wheat in 1939 was the best pre-war year for native wheat production, this quantity was still only one-third of the nation's requirements.[47] With the outbreak of the Second World War and the Emergency, increased wheat production was seen not only of paramount importance to Ireland's self-sufficiency in foodstuffs but also central to its national security and survival as a neutral state. Ryan employed all types of media to induce farmers to 'grow more wheat', ranging from 'a campaign of advertising and propaganda in the press, by pictorial posters, cinematograph displays – with the aim of having 700,000 acres of wheat grown' (Fig. 71).[48] One notable poster campaign by the Department of Agriculture in 1942 was widely exhibited 'on roadside hoardings, in railway stations, creameries, seed merchants' premises, National Schools, Post offices, Garda Stations and licensed premises'.[49] The same year the Catholic church was enlisted in the campaign with the bishops calling for greater food production.[50]

Despite Ryan's campaign, the introduction of compulsory tillage in 1940 was to create 'tension between centre and periphery', unsettling relationships between state and farmer. Lampooned in satirical magazines (Fig. 72), compulsory tillage was to remain a contentious issue throughout the Emergency as shortages increased, and tillage stipulations became more stringent and punitive. The mandatory, arable quota on farmland was introduced in 1940 at one-eight; this was increased to one-quarter by late 1941. By 1944 the limit on the size of farms that came under the Compulsory Tillage Order was reduced from ten to five acres with the arable quota on

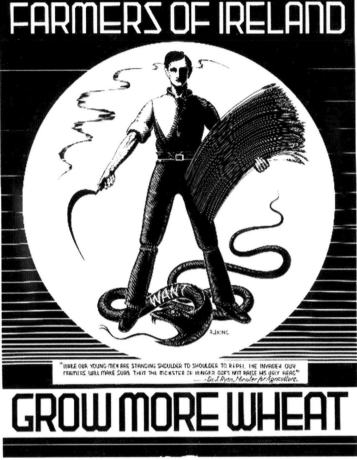

71 Poster from 1942 by R.J. King encouraging farmers to grow more wheat. Courtesy of Dr James Ryan, grandson of Minister for Agriculture, Dr Ryan.

farmland increased to three-eights. The maximum penalty for failing to comply with tillage orders increased from £100 to £500 in 1942.[51]

Bryce Evans takes the view that the implementation of compulsory tillage by the Department of Agriculture was a 'hard-headed top-down approach' implemented through the twin prongs of 'counsel with coercion', graphically described in the Seanád as compulsory tillage enforced 'at the point of a bayonet'. He argues that relations between farmers and the state were significantly fractured 'by the widespread perception that compulsory tillage was foisted on them by a brutish and heedless Dublin bureaucracy'. This was

72 Cartoon from the front cover of *Dublin Opinion*, February, 1942, parodying the stringency of the government's compulsory tillage order. 'Billy is it? Then may I ask if you have read the Compulsory Tillage Order?'

"Billy is it? Then may I ask if you have read the Compulsory Tillage Order?"

further compounded when Department officers were empowered 'to enter on to and take possession of holdings of any farmers who failed to comply with their quota'; it was in effect a 'bold threat' which 'belied the cosy ruralism of government propaganda'.[52]

Compulsory tillage not only created tensions between the state and farmers but also revealed divisions within the farming community. Evans maintains that compulsory tillage disproportionately affected farmers in the lower socio-economic bands and estimates that between 1941 and 1945 the state dispossessed on average 305 holdings per year. He suggests, during the 1940s, the non-compliant farmer on trial had become an alternative symbol to the small farmer as noble ploughman depicted on the pound note, and reflected the state's 'condescension towards its rural peripheries and those who inhabited them'. This was undoubtedly reinforced by de Valera's warning 'Till or Go to Jail', coupled with Lemass' enthusiasm for land dispossession and his view that 'land policy must be geared towards ownership based on ability to work the land' through the 'elimination of incompetent or lazy farmers'.[53]

The degree to which the state can coerce a community into a particular course of action is dependent on whether or not the campaign of coercion is perceived as oppressive by the community concerned or a necessary evil which must be endured for the greater good and the survival of the community and the state. Evans claims that despite the spectre of dispossession the majority of the farming community regarded compulsory tillage during the Emergency as 'a last resort' – a painful but exceptional necessity of wartime conditions.[54] Irish farmers responded to the call to grow more wheat by extending the acreage under wheat to 662,498 by 1945, more than two-and-a-half times the 1939 figure.[55]

The men behind the plough

> Turn down the green, O man who ploughs:
> Guide thou the plough with sharpened share!
> Turn up the brown to sapphire skies!
> Mankind on thee for bread relies.[56]

During the 1930s and 1940s the widespread introduction of tractors into Ireland was restricted by the effects of the Economic War with Britain and the Emergency. In Northern Ireland, despite the increase in the number of tractors from 550 in 1939 to 7,300 by 1945, horses remained the main source of draught power on farms until the late fifties (Fig. 73). During this period horse ploughing remained the dominant form of tillage north and south in Ireland, and with the 'grow more wheat' campaign the ploughmen took on the status of national heroes and soldiers in the fight for self-sufficiency in bread. In Dáil Éireann, Deputy Bolton proclaimed:

> It does not matter what manoeuvres we have, what war weapons we have, there is really only one weapon of defence for the neutrality and freedom of this country, and that is the plough.
> The greatest soldier in this country is the man behind the plough. He is the greatest defender of our Liberties and of our neutrality, and is saving the state.[57]

Winners of the National Ploughing Championships were held in high esteem at both local and national level. One such ploughman was Michael Redmond

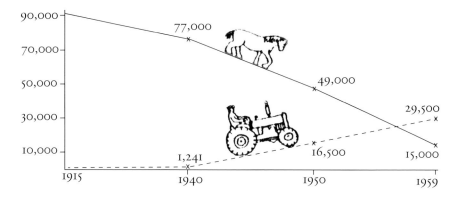

73 Northern Ireland Ministry of Agriculture graph showing the rise of tractor power and the decline of horse power between 1915 and 1959.

from Ballagh, Oulart, County Wexford (Fig. 74), who won the national title in 1932, was champion ploughman for two decades and had a ballad composed about him which was 'sung or recited with cheers and gusto throughout the land'.[58]

Discussing the symbolic linkage of community with the past Cohen takes the position derivative of Malinowski:

> People's models of the past are a 'charter' for contemporary action whose legitimacy derives from its very association with the cultural past.[59]

De Valera painted Ireland's future as lying in a rural idyll of a 'countryside bright with cosy homesteads … with the romping of sturdy children, the contests of athletic youths, and the laughter of comely maidens',[60] at the head of which is the idealised ploughman farmer as depicted on the Irish pound note. At the National Ploughing Championships in 1941 the *Irish Times* reported that 'Mr de Valera remarked to Michael Redmond that it had always been his wish, since he was a boy, to use a plough'.[61] Taking Cohen's view, expressed above, de Valera was publicly linking himself with the rural community, its cultural past, and from his perspective legitimising the state policy of compulsory tillage. Ironically, two years later it was alleged in Dáil Éireann that 'Michael Redmond was forced by bad remuneration to leave the land and sell gravel in Dublin'.[62] The allegation was strongly refuted by the

74 A crowd of earnest spectators watch champion ploughman Michael Redmond turn a winning furrow at the 1936 National Ploughing Championships in Tullamore, Co. Offaly (*Irish Times*, 20 February 1936).

75 J.J. Egan, winner of the 1954 horse ploughing championship, opening his winning plot at the World Ploughing Championships in Killarney. (Photo: Muckross Research Library.)

Minister for Agriculture, Dr Ryan, who hailed Redmond as 'a national figure'. Epitomising 'the spirit of Ireland' and the ploughman farmer with generational ties to the land, Ryan described Redmond as having:

> … lived all his live on a very small farm of 25 acres and made a very good living. He reared ten children has now two sons, as well as himself, who are ploughmen. They are happy on that farm and are not depending on the drawing of sand or anything else like that.[63]

The allegation was subsequently withdrawn.

76 Dan McKendry ploughing with his Moyarget swing plough at the Ballycastle Ploughing Society's annual match, *c*.1930s.

Three horse ploughing greats from the Abbeydorney Ploughing Society who brought All-Ireland honours to the parish and County Kerry were John Joe Egan (Fig. 75), Patrick O'Mahony, from Aulane, and Patrick J.P. Shanahan, from Ballylahive. During their ploughing careers they were said to be 'as well-known as any member of the Kerry Football team of their day', and 'made the name of Abbeydorney famous to fellow ploughmen throughout the length and breadth of Ireland'.[64]

From Moyarget, County Antrim, the late Patrick McKillop's hero ploughman was local man Dan McKendry who ploughed with a swing plough made by McKillop's father who was the local blacksmith. Dan McKendry's most treasured trophy was the Succession Cup awarded by the Ballycastle Ploughing Society. He had the plough irons set for the winning match by McKillop's father. Elated by Dan McKendry's ploughing Pat McKillop remembered 'every furrow was sitting dead on the rule ... the whole world couldn't have beat Dan McKendry that day' (Fig. 76). Despite coming third in his class, for the McKillops, Dan McKendry's greatest performance with the swing plough was in 1938 at the first International Ploughing Championships held in Northern Ireland. Up against 'all the champion men from England and Scotland' who were using the most technically advanced horse ploughs of the time, equipped with an array of attachments for cutting, pressing and defining the furrow slice, Patrick McKillop's father proclaimed, 'it's manpower against machinery'.[65] Coming third in a David and Goliath contest was as good as victory, if not a moral victory for the McKillops.

Horse ploughing matches at national and local level were primarily all-male affairs with competitors and spectators predominantly made up of men and boys. The earliest horse ploughing match (known to the authors) with a female competitor was a local match held near Limavady, County Derry, in 1923. Its novelty value is highlighted by the star billing given to the competitor, Jemima Quigley, in the *Belfast Newsletter*'s report:

CO. DERRY PLOUGHING MATCH
Woman Competitor Successful

At the 29th annual ploughing competitions held on Thursday under the auspices of the Boveva and Roe Valley Farming Society, the first place in chill [wheel] ploughing class was won by Mr W.J. Quigley, whose plough was held by his sister, Miss Jemima Quigley, who displayed skill quite equal to her rivals of the other sex. She also won four special prizes for the best 'backs' for the best 'hints' for the best taped horses, and third place in the best groomed competition.[66]

Interestingly, Jemima Quigley was competing in the same class as male competitors. In the 1950s, when women were finally allowed to compete at national level in the tractor ploughing section, they had to compete in a separate class from the male competitors. The National Ploughing Association called the women's section the Farmerette Class and the Northern Ireland Ploughing Association named it the Ladies Class. The only other female competitor known to the authors, who was recorded at the end of the heyday of horse ploughing, was an unnamed competitor photographed at a local ploughing match near Carndonagh, County Donegal, in the 1950s (Fig. 77).

Women, however, did play a vital nurturing role at local matches, where they provided food and drink for competitors, usually in the form of tea and sandwiches (Fig. 78).

77 Unnamed female competitor adjusts the 'wee' wheel of her plough at a local match near Carndonagh, Co. Donegal, in the 1950s (courtesy of the Derry Journal Ltd), from Helen Meehan, 'Donegal Women in History' in Jim Mac Laughlin and Sean Beattie (eds), *Atlas of County Donegal* (Cork: Cork University Press, 2013), p. 391.

Looking back

The mechanisation of farming forged ahead during the late forties and fifties with the inevitable demise of horse ploughing and the growth of tractor ploughing. By the late 1970s support for horse ploughing had declined, particularly at national level. Entrants to the horse section were so few in the Northern Ireland International Ploughing Championships that the rules were relaxed. Bertie Hanna who competed in many international championships remembered:

78 (*Top*) A welcome break for
competitors when tea arrived at
the Craigantlet and Dundonald
Ploughing Society match at
Ballycultra, County Down.
(*Right*) Mr W. Ferguson, secretary
and competitor, takes a break
(*Belfast Newsletter*, January 1935).

> They relaxed themselves in the rules because the competitors was so
> little at the time there. I remember when there was only maybe three
> ploughing at the International so nobody bothered with the rules.[67]

During the late 1980s horse ploughing matches enjoyed a revival and renewed
interest which continues today. However, the strict enforcement of rules at
matches remains problematic. James Musgrave, horse ploughing judge as well
as ploughman from County Down, expressed the following opinion about the

rules and the context in which horse ploughing matches take place in the current revival:

> Ach well you've got to go easy on them. You've got to remember its not like the old days. In the old days those horses would have been working everyday, ploughing and working round the farm. So they were used to it, it was second nature to them. Nowadays, people keeps them for a bit of a pastime. Most of those horses only get a bit of a run round the field the day before a match. Some of them not even that. So they're bound to be a bit fresh, jump around a bit and step in the furrows and that. You've got allow for that.[68]

The definition of horse ploughing as a pastime emphasises the changing role of the horse on the farm, from that of a working animal to that of an animal used for leisure pursuits, which reflect and maintain a link with a past farming life.[69] The recent revival of horse ploughing matches is regarded by some as a reaffirmation of the farming community's connection with a past in which farming is perceived as being more in tune with nature and the life cycle of birth, death and regeneration. This is echoed in the Abbeydorney Ploughing Society's remembrance of past horse ploughmen in the society.

> To see them in action was an example of the perfect harmony between a man and his team of horses. No more will their voices echo the ploughing fields, or the creaking harness, and subdued rattle of the ploughing chains of their horses be heard. During their ploughing life they had turned the soil to the sun in several counties in Ireland. The soil is now their mantle as they rest in dignity and peace.[70]

James Musgrave, emphasising the bond between ploughman and horse, and the detrimental effect of the tractor on the soil, maintained:

> Oh aye you can't have a relationship with a tractor. You never get cold behind a pair of horses and what's more the horses don't compact the soil the same way the tractors do. The tractors are faster though, its all speed now.[71]

Some modern supporters of the working horse see it not only as having a symbolic linkage with the past, but regard its resurrection on the farm as essential for the future of sustainable farming. Irish Draught Horse enthusiast Murt Fitzgerald from west Cork, who works the family farm, like his father and grandfather before him, regards the working horse as the power unit of the future and argues:

> There should … be at least one horse on every farm to supplement the tractor and do the many jobs that the horse does best … I think we must get back to a more natural and sustainable type of food production – and the draught horse (in my case the Irish Draught Horse) is a fundamental part of that re-think.[72]

One aspect of collective identity shared by older ploughmen that rooted them in the farming community was their generational ties to horse ploughing. Horse ploughing was perceived as being 'in the blood', with knowledge of ploughing passed between generations. An area where the passing of knowledge between generations is symbolically expressed is in the changing role of the members of the plough team. A plough team is usually made up of two members – the ploughman and the helper. Entry for the competition is made in the ploughman's name, who is referred to as 'holding' the plough – a term used at early nineteenth-century matches mentioned earlier. When the father wants to 'pass over the plough' to the son, the son's name is entered as 'holding' the plough. The role of helper is then usually taken over by the father or another son.[73] Two veteran ploughmen, Bertie Hanna and John Andrews, acknowledged the importance of their fathers' tutelage in the skills of horse ploughing. Bertie recounted:

> I never got away from the horses. I was born with horses. I never left them. I was ploughing from I was ten you know … My father taught me to drill [plough]. The thing was done everyday and you picked it up as you went along.[74]

Bertie's brother Lindsay is also a keen horse ploughman.

The late John Andrews lived on the family farm near Toomebridge, County Antrim. His father, renowned for his ploughing skills, was known as the 'one-armed ploughman' due to the loss of the lower part of his left arm in the First World War. John took great pride in his father having ploughed at the first International Ploughing Championships in 1938 (Fig. 79) continuing to

Mr R J Andrews, Toombridge, the one armed ploughman at work watched by a large gallery

79 John Andrews' father, R.J. Andrews, the 'one armed ploughman', competing at the first International Ploughing Championships in Northern Ireland in 1938.

80 John Andrews, aged 13, watched by an 'interested audience' did 'splendid work' at Castledawson Ploughing Society's first annual ploughing match near Castledawson, County Derry (*Belfast Newsletter*, 19 February 1936).

plough with the harness his father used at the International Competition.[75] As a young lad in the 1930s John competed at local matches with his father's horses and plough (Fig. 80).

Bertie and John willingly shared their knowledge of horse ploughing and experience of competitive ploughing with the authors and were central to the establishment of a horse ploughing match at the Ulster Folk and Transport Museum in the late 1980s. Well known at ploughing matches near and far, Bertie helped ensure the lasting success of the match by enticing an ever expanding number of contestants and helpers from the horse ploughing community to the museum. Now under the control of farm manager and horse ploughman Robert Berry, the future of the museum match looks assured (along with a little advice from Bertie and their chum Ivan in the hospitality room).

One family where horse ploughing skills still abound is the King family from County Louth. Head of the King family, All-Ireland ploughing champion, Gerry, recalled 'his father being a great ploughman who would eat sleep and talk ploughing'. Ensuring that horse ploughing will carry on down the generations, Gerry's two sons, Gerard and David, have carried on the tradition, winning All-Ireland titles themselves. The family's best years for titles were from 2002 to 2004 when they won the senior, open and under-40s classes for three years in a row.[76]

During the current revival women have tended to participate in matches in a supportive role as helper – harnessing, leading and holding the horses. There have been individual appearances by female competitors such as Margaret Johnston, who held the plough for John Andrews at a museum match in the early 1990s.[77] In west Cork in 2009 at the 55th Cahermore Ploughing Association's match, Annie Prendergast was said have 'put on a brilliant display'.[78] Recently, in 2013, Caroline Fahy from Galway, with her uncle Joe as helper (Fig. 81), competed in the All-Ireland under-40s horse class to gain a very creditable 106 points.[79] Hopefully, in the near future, with the help of farming families and friends, women will become a formidable force in the horse ploughing community.

In the recent revival of horse ploughing matches symbolic bonding between the state and the farming community continues. With the ongoing importance of agriculture to the national economy senior state figures, following in de Valera's footsteps, have continued to attend the National Ploughing Championships. In the recent economic recession the agricultural sector is one that has been bearing 'green shoots'. Keen to be associated with economic success and symbolically support the sector, Taoiseach Enda Kenny attended the National Ploughing Championships and publicly reaffirmed his Mayo farming roots (Fig. 82) at the horse ploughing class.

81 Caroline Fahy from Galway, with uncle Joe helping, competes in the under-40s horse class at the 2013 National Ploughing Championships.

82 Taoiseach Enda Kenny 'holds' the plough at the 2013 National Ploughing Championships.

83 Self-proclaimed 'cultchie', Co. Clare Rose of Tralee, Marie Donnellan, pictured with a pair of plough horses at the 2013 County Clare Ploughing Championships.

President Higgins, waxing lyrical at the 2013 championships, remarked that it evoked the 'rich symbolism of renewal and fruitfulness' and 'conjured up a world that reminded him of his formative years living on a small farm in Newmarket-on-Fergus, County Clare'.[80] Statesmen were not the only public figures from Clare to attend ploughing matches and affirm their rural roots. 2013 County Clare Rose of Tralee, Marie Donnellan, also from Newmarket-on-Fergus, attended the County Clare Ploughing Championships as her first official duty.

Photographed beside the horses of ploughman Jim Cronin from Bridgetown (Fig. 83), and no doubt to the delight of onlookers, Marie proudly boasted: 'as a self-proclaimed "cultchie" and a big follower of the ploughing championships, it was amazing to attend the event this year as the Clare Rose.'[81]

The farming community have regarded horse ploughing matches not just as competitive events but as major social occasions. In Cahermore, the local match was so popular the creamery gave its staff a half-day off. The event

84 Tossing the sheaf competition at the 1939 National Ploughing Championships in Killarney.

attracted a wide range of spectators, including local TDs, agricultural officials and local media.[82] At national level the social importance of ploughing matches was quickly realised. In 1937, it was decided to have a dance and supper on the eve of the match and a dinner dance on the night of the match.[83] Games and other activities reflecting rural life were also incorporated. At the 1939 championships in Killarney events included 'horse-shoeing, sheaf-tossing (Fig. 84), estimating the weight of pigs and bullocks, judging the milk yield of cows, and other such attractions, including a tug-o'-war contest between the various counties'.[84] Many of these activities still take place at local ploughing competitions and reaffirm the cultural past of the farming community.

85 Dolly McRoberts helped by her late sister Isobel and sister Nettie give out tea and sandwiches to veteran horse ploughman Bertie Hanna and assembled friends and followers of the plough at the Ulster Folk and Transport Museum Ploughing Match.

An integral part of social interaction at horse ploughing matches is the 'craic' and includes all those elements of social intercourse such as a 'good gossip', 'having a laugh' and remembering past friends. Usually at its peak when the tea and sandwiches are brought round to the competitors (Fig. 85) or in the 'hospitality' spaces provided, the 'craic' helps make ploughing matches into a social occasion that bonds ploughmen together. This is fittingly reflected in Bertie Hanna's view of horse ploughing matches as occasions 'for making friends for life and for ever, the best you can know, an odd pint, what more can you ask'.[85]

Chapter 7

Celebrating farming history: heritage events, heritage centres and museums

Ploughing matches are only one way in which country people engage with their past. For more than a century, Irish country festivals have staged re-enactments of rural heritage, ancient and modern, in an increasing range of events. Some old festivals, such as the Puck Fair in Killorgin, County Kerry (Fig. 87), or the Oul' Lammas Fair in Ballycastle, County Antrim, are major tourist events, and attracting local and international visitors is an explicit aim of the many rural festivals organised each summer. Some of the newer events make little claim to be celebrating farming traditions. One of the most imaginative festivals in this category is held in Ballyjamesduff, County Cavan, where an International Pork Festival was established in the 1990s, 'mainly due to a nearby pork-rendering factory regularly supplying a large amount of pork for use in the town festival'.[1] The festival includes demonstrations of crafts and skills, but in 2013, the programme was designed with a gleeful disregard for the spirit of seriousness:

Kosher Kraziness (a kosher food eating contest)
The Pig Run (similar to the Running of the Bulls, but with boars instead of bulls)
The Swine and Cheese Party (a more cultural Pork and Cheese tasting party)
Grills Gone Wild (a pig and pig-farmer beauty contest)
The Olympigs (a day of track and field events for pig farmers)
The Speaking in Pig Latin Debate Competition (people must speak as long as they can in Pig Latin)
Pig Racing (pigs racing with knitted jockeys attached to their backs).[2]

Festivals which have more serious aspirations often concentrate on one aspect of farming, a crop or particular breed of livestock, or vintage farm machinery. For example, Trim, County Meath, has an annual haymaking festival, while the Boley Fair in Hilltown, County Down, celebrates traditions of sheep farming and booleying in the Mourne Mountains. Some of the biggest events focus on vintage machinery, include tractors and portable threshing machines. One of the most impressive of these festivals is the

86 'After the Grain was Harvested' by Philip Flanagan, acrylic on linen (2011).

Moynalty Steam Threshing Event in County Meath (Fig. 88). The festival, which was first held in 1976, has an annual attendance of around 30,000 visitors. There is a fun fair, set and step dancing, and cookery demonstrations, but the main focus is on the threshing and related activities such as cutting grain with a horse-drawn reaper, mowing with scythes and a rare demonstration of reaping with a sickle (Fig. 89). There is a large display of old farm implements and other activities include twisting straw rope and making mud turf. The festival successfully provides both fun and education, a great day out and a learning experience.

Festivals and events usually last from between one and three days; publicly funded, and commercial museums and heritage centres, present aspects of rural history in longer term displays. As with all other aspects of history and heritage, the meaning and significance of these displays has changed through time. Like ploughing matches, the educational goals of the earliest farming exhibitions were directed towards the future rather than the past. In 1733, for example, a display of new farm implements was set up in a vault of the Irish parliament, and in 1781 the Dublin Society opened a museum in Poolbeg Street where experimental farm implements were displayed and sold. As with ploughing matches and other rural events, the change in focus from future to past came with the sense of a way of life threatened by modernity. Displays which examined farming history and heritage were closely linked with the development of folklife studies, discussed below, and with a sense of nostalgia for a lost world, real or imagined.

Planning an exhibition of this kind immediately raises a number of theoretical and practical issues, and the quality of the resulting display largely depends on how exhibition planners engage with these. Some of the issues raised can seem very abstract, far removed from the practicalities of tasks such as cleaning artefacts and writing captions, but it is important that curators are at least aware of them, and of the conceptual muddles that can arise if they are ignored.

Is there such a thing as real history?

In the first chapter of this book, we outlined some of the issues arising from the use of oral evidence about the past, but scholars have asked even more fundamental questions about history, including the most fundamental of all: how can we know anything at all about the past? This question became popular in some academic circles several decades ago with the rise of what is

PUCK FAIR.KILLORGLIN.CO.KERRY.7640.W.L.

87 Puck Fair, Killorglin, County Kerry. This fair, held annually every 10 August, goes back at least to the early seventeenth century, but the display of a goat as King of the Fair has led to speculation that its roots might be much more ancient. (Photo: National Library of Ireland, Lawrence coll., 7640.)

usually referred to as post-modernism. It is easy to understand why museum staff, faced with the practicalities of putting on an exhibition, might be tempted to dismiss the debate as an esoteric mind game, an issue which should only be discussed in the rarefied world of the philosopher's study. We all know that the past really existed; if we didn't, the simplest activities like going home after a day's work would not be possible. (We wouldn't know what or where 'home' was.) However, at a fundamental level, being aware of the implications of the question can make the difference between good and bad history. Ignoring it can lead to interpretations loaded with unexamined value judgements and prejudices. Coming from a social science background, we have been surprised at a notion among some historians that all we need to do is find the facts, and the account we make using them will be objective and true, that the facts speak for themselves. When we look at some of the ways we find out about history, and how we present our findings, it is clear that this is

88 The threshing festival in Moynalty, County Meath, 2013. This festival successfully combines a lot of entertainment with a deep respect for farming heritage.

89 Reaping grain with a sickle, demonstrated at Moynalty in 2013 by Francis Doherty of Trostan, County Fermanagh.

far from true, and that unintentional distortion can enter even the most earnest presentations of historic documents, objects and buildings. David Lowenthal has argued that these distortions are inevitable.

> Simply to appreciate a relic, let alone embellish and imitate it, affects its form or our impressions … New interests and needs, new memories and forgettings force each generation to revise what relics it notices and how to interpret them … history is continually altered.[3]

Faced with this complication, some museum staff have taken its implications to extremes, and joined cynics of the 'history is bunk' kind, amusing themselves (and some erudite visitors) with ironic play, mixing different aspects of history together, in clever but absurd confusion. Our view is, however, that while such confusion can be used very creatively in films, literature and computer games, allowing it to shape historical research is an abdication of responsibility. Philosophers have known for thousands of years that seeing beyond the distortions created by fantasy and illusion to find what is really real is incredibly difficult. In one of Plato's most famous metaphors, people in a cave look at its back wall, and conclude that the shadows cast by a fire behind them are reality. Some, however, become aware of the fire, then the light outside the cave, and a few even identify the ultimate source of this light, the sun. The challenge is to go beyond the shadows of appearance, to find reality.[4] Our obligation to search for truth, including historical truth, does not disappear because the task is so difficult. This sense of obligation is shared by most serious thinkers. The anti-platonic Jean-Paul Sartre, for example, saw all knowledge as constantly being reconstructed, but argued that we must work at producing history that from our own historical position we cannot go beyond.[5] The meanings we give to history change, but the valid data that should inform our historical understanding do not. We know that the facts do not speak for themselves, but even committed postmodern historians must allow for the authority of evidence.[6] Eric Hobsbawm has expressed this very clearly.

> The point from which historians must start, however far from it they end, is the fundamental … distinction between establishable fact and fiction, between historical statements based on evidence and subject to evidence and those which are not … Either Elvis Presley is dead or he isn't …

Relativism will not do in history any more than in law courts. Whether the accused in a murder trial is or is not guilty depends on the assessment of old-fashioned positivist evidence … Any innocent readers who find themselves in the dock will do well to appeal to it. It is the lawyers for the guilty ones who will fall back on post-modern lines of defence.[7]

Museums and objects

In most museums, the evidence for past lives is still based on collections of objects. Museums and heritage centres rely more and more on multi-media techniques to interpret their subject areas, but objects are still central to how museums are defined. Collections of old farm implements in Ireland range from objects accumulated by individuals, often displayed in farm outbuildings, to national museum collections, north and south. At both these extremes we often find obsessive attempts to collect every variant of an implement's design, perhaps a 'crank' approach, but one which is usually driven by at least some interest in assessing an object's historical significance (Figs. 90 and 91). In contrast to this obsession with detail, however, there are heritage centres and 'experiences' that often show a worrying disdain for even the most basic information. Some years ago, two English comics did a television sketch in which they played the part of countrywomen who ripped off gullible incomers, selling them 'old' objects such as an iron-toothed rabbit trap painted in white gloss and decorated with dried flowers. Some displays in Irish heritage centres bring this to mind. Large brightly painted objects are set around as props, relics of old Ireland; the fact that they are the products of heavy industrial foundries in places such as Huddersfield or Chicago is unnoticed and, of course, unrecorded. It was the proliferation of this sort of heritage attraction that gave impetus to the drive, directed by Ireland's Heritage Council, to develop criteria for museum registration, which focus on development and care of collections. To be recognised as a museum, an institution must demonstrate that its collections are researched, developed, interpreted, and held in trust for public benefit.

Seamus Heaney has described the potential of objects to provide a direct link with the past.

90 Reaper seats displayed in Graham's farm, Ardagh, County Donegal.

To an imaginative person, an inherited object like a garden seat is not just an object, an antique, an item on an inventory; rather it becomes a point of entry into a common emotional ground of memory and belonging. It can transmit the climate of a lost world and keep alive in us a domestic intimacy with realities that otherwise might have vanished. The more we are surrounded by such objects and are attentive to them, the more richly and contentedly we dwell in our own lives.[8]

In the following discussion, we will examine why it is important to collect and document farm artefacts, and give examples of good practice that we have encountered (including, happily, some heritage centres which, in contradiction to the comments just made, take their educational role very seriously).

91 Spades made in McMahon's spade mill, Clones, now in the collection of the Ulster Folk and Transport Museum.

Linking objects and techniques to social relations

Great social theorists, like Marx and Durkheim, made important observations about the place of technology in society, and some leading anthropologists, such as Marvin Harris and Claude Lévi-Strauss, have also attempted to include techniques and artefacts in their theoretical discussions of how different elements of society connect with one another.[9] However, when we try to apply these grand statements to detailed case studies, the generalisations made by the theorists are often too abstract to cast much light on specific cases. The gap between the big ideas and an individual piece of machinery became very obvious when we began working with the agricultural collections in the Ulster Folk and Transport Museum in the 1970s. The tangled rows of rusting implements confronting us seemed to be very far removed from the significant relationships identified by any social science theory that we knew of, or the romantic 'cultural essence' models of the past which underpinned a lot of folklife analysis at the time.

Some Irish anthropological studies have attempted to include accounts of the environment and working lives of the people being researched. For example, in the 1930s, Arensberg and Kimball discussed systems of land-holding, crop rotations, and typical days' work undertaken by members of farming families in their research in County Clare. This account provides a useful context or backdrop in which the social relationships examined can be placed, but it does not show any close articulation between these social relationships and artefacts and techniques. This criticism could be made of a lot of anthropological research in Ireland. Fortunately, however, there are exceptions, including some research into relationships of mutual help between farmers. Some of these studies provide good examples of ways in which social ties can be expressed or affected by farming methods; Rosemary Harris' research in County Tyrone in the 1950s is one of the best instances of this.

In the case studies recorded by Harris, some local farmers started or stopped working together because of changes in the machinery they used. One farmer, Paul Jamison, had 'swopped' help with his uncle for some years, borrowing his horses at busy times, but he eventually got his own team of two working horses, and when his three sons were sufficiently grown up to help on the farm, he ended his working relationship with his uncle. He also began to work instead with his brother-in-law Fred Richards, who could borrow Paul's horses in return for providing his own labour. This lasted until Paul bought a tractor, which meant that Fred could no longer exchange help on an equal basis. Paul's cousin Bill, however, could still make a valuable contribution, because of his experience with farm contract work, which had given him skills as a tractor driver and a mechanic. Harris shows convincingly that it was not surprising that he replaced Fred as Paul's swopping partner.[10]

The implications of changing implements and techniques are quite clear here, and sometimes even more detailed analysis of farming methods are relevant. We saw in chapter 3 how one farmer took revenge on his neighbour by the way he hitched a team of two horses to a set of harrows. In another instance we recorded in County Antrim, a blacksmith was accused of expressing his sectarian prejudices in the different ways he set the irons (share and coulter) on competitors' ploughs before a ploughing match.[11] These two examples can only be made intelligible through a detailed understanding of the technology involved. However, in both instances there was no necessary connection between the techniques and the social relationships involved. Neighbourly help could take many forms, or revenge could be taken and prejudice expressed in many ways. In general, what strikes us about the application of technology in Irish farming during the last three centuries is the flexibility and inventiveness with which farmers used social ties to ensure

92 A County Down family preparing linen thread for weaving in 1783. (Etching by W. Hincks.)

access to new methods. As we have seen, expensive machinery like a threshing machine could be borrowed in return for labour, hired as necessary, or bought co-operatively. At the level of hand tools and manual techniques, flexibility is even more obvious. For example, one person could carry out all the work involved in planting potatoes. However, it was also common for two people to work together, at either side of a cultivation ridge, or for groups of several people to work together, planting a crop for each member of the group in return. In the absence of this kind of help, farmers could hire workers, such as the spailpíní (spalpeens) described earlier. It is clear that, at present, we do not have a method of linking detailed descriptions of specific artefacts and techniques to broad general statements about how technology and society mesh together. However, this does not reduce the value of historic artefacts. The great social theorists were right. There is a systematic, albeit very complex and open-ended relationship between technology, the division of labour and other social relations. There are examples that illustrate this. Irish farmers understand that techniques selected have implications for other farming operations; how you plant a crop affects how you care for it while it is growing and how it can be harvested. In some instances, this can increase understanding of the relationship between techniques, the division of labour, the system of landholding and the system of trade. The development of the linen industry in eighteenth-century Ulster provides a neat example of this. Linen production at the time was a labour-intensive home industry, so it made sense to organise production in small farming units, which could utilise family labour. (A small farm and a big family was ideal.) (Fig. 92) This helps us to understand the spread of very small farms in Ulster during the late eighteenth and early nineteenth centuries, and why farms remained small, even by Irish standards, until well within living memory.

In this book, we have tried to use some approaches developed in social anthropology. As with all the social sciences, fashions in theory come and go in anthropology, sometimes very quickly. However, as we pointed out in an earlier chapter, one lasting achievement of the subject is that it is based on listening to what people actually say, and what they actually do. Irish country people, past and present, certainly spend more time discussing work and technology than they do in discussing, for example, the concept of community. Museum-based interpretations should start from a similar point.

CASE STUDIES

Museums dealing with rural life, or 'folklife', have proliferated throughout Ireland during the last fifty years, from Sneem in County Kerry to Kilmacrennan in County Donegal. These are often intended for tourists, but growing interest in local history has meant that even in areas where tourism is not so important, such as Fivemiletown in County Tyrone, local artefacts have been collected and displayed. Some of these developments include outdoor museums, where vernacular buildings taken from elsewhere, or replicas, have been built and furnished to show the way of life in the past. A small, but very evocative outdoor museum has been established at Glencolumkille in Donegal, while at the other end of the scale, Bunratty Folk Park in County Clare is well-established as one of Ireland's leading tourist attractions. Several other museums with outdoor displays will be discussed below.

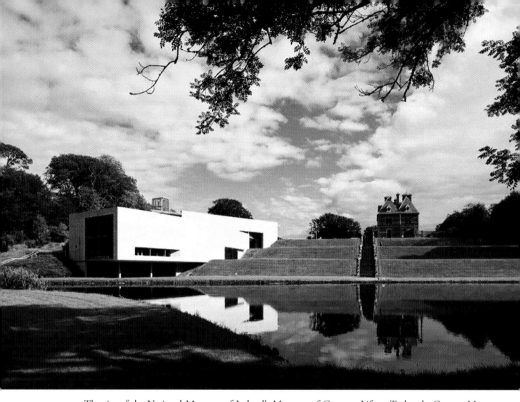

93 The site of the National Museum of Ireland's Museum of Country Life at Turlough, County Mayo, showing the new exhibition galleries and the nineteenth-century house. (Photo: National Museum of Ireland.)

94 Part of the farming display at the National Museum of Ireland's Museum of Country Life. (Photo: National Museum of Ireland.)

Museum of Country Life, Turlough Park, County Mayo

Turlough Park is part of the National Museum of Ireland, the home of the museum's Folklife division since 2001 (Fig. 93). Folklife material was first displayed in the museum's Kildare Street galleries in 1937. The curatorial approach to research, collection and display is based on the study of ethnology as developed in northern Europe in the early twentieth century. While the assumptions and methodology of this approach have been criticised in recent

95 Séamas MacPhilib, Curator of Agriculture in the National Museum of Ireland.

decades, one of its ongoing strengths was that it focused on locally-made 'vernacular' artefacts (Fig. 94). The resulting collection of farm implements is of both national and international importance, and its significance is emphasized by the respect with which it is treated in documentation, conservation and display.

Dr Séamas MacPhilib, the museum's curator of agriculture, was trained as a folklorist (Fig. 95). His research on landlordism in Donegal shows the potential of folklore collections to deepen understanding of the aspirations and values of people whose lives would otherwise have been unrecorded, an approach to research which is in line with the one taken in this book.[12]

Ulster Folk and Transport Museum

This museum, which opened at Cultra in County Down in 1958, followed earlier Scandinavian models, and specifically the approach taken by Hazelius, when he founded the museum at Skansen in Sweden in the 1891. Formal gallery displays were used to provide a historic context for exhibit buildings erected in an open-air display area. The buildings at Cultra had originally been located throughout the nine historic counties of Ulster. They were dismantled and rebuilt in the museum's outdoor park, an area of around 25 hectares which had been part of the demesne of a Big House beside Belfast Lough. Cultra Manor, which dates from around 1900, stands in dramatic contrast to the buildings brought in to the museum, most of which are rural dwellings, furnished to represent the way of life in Ulster around 1900. The spaces between the vernacular buildings have been landscaped in an attempt to reflect their original settings, and some sort of representation of farming life was considered necessary to make this convincing. When we started work in the museum in 1975, this representation consisted of six badly behaved donkeys.

Our first tentative move towards establishing a 'living farm' in the museum was to organise a demonstration of horse ploughing. The ploughed ground was then sown with winter wheat, and harvesting this with a horse drawn reaper established an annual cycle of tillage, which we gradually expanded to include potatoes, oats and hay, the most common crops in Ulster in 1900. We also brought livestock into the museum, concentrating on surviving Irish breeds such as Kerry and Irish Moiled cattle, Mourne and Galway sheep, and Irish Draft horses. We also obtained feral goats from County Fermanagh, Large White pigs, and a mixture of poultry breeds.

96 Robert Berry, Farm Manager, and Robbie Hannan, Curator of Agriculture and Folklife, in the Ulster Folk and Transport Museum.

We were, of course, playing at farming. We did not have to keep a family alive, or make money, but even the early experiments brought some realities of farming life into sharp focus. The inexorable cycle of crop production was one of these, and the need for round-the-clock supervision of livestock. Fortunately, the museum management saw the potential of the farm as a visitor attraction, and in the early 1980s resources were provided to employ a farm manager and farm labourer, with some part-time back-up staff (Fig. 96). This allowed curatorial staff to develop the ploughing match described in chapter six (Fig. 97), and other major events days, including an annual Rare Breeds Sale and Show, which involved the auction and display of hundreds of farm animals.

The practicalities of farming were extremely useful for us as agricultural curators. We became familiar with a lot of relevant techniques, such as ridge making, drill cultivation, and harvesting flax. Discussions about the uses of different types of straw in nineteenth-century farming texts made a lot of sense

97 Robert Berry working with a slipe in the Corradreenan farmyard in the Ulster Folk and Transport Museum.

98 A replica of an eighteenth-century long-beamed Irish plough made by Seamus O'Kane of Dungiven being tested at the Ulster Folk and Transport Museum's ploughing match in 1988.

after we had worked at harvesting and threshing grain, and we began to understand some basic rules for tending animals, especially when they needed hooves clipped or when they were in labour. We became confident enough at crop production to try to replicate some older farming techniques such as growing oats on spade ridges or trying out a reproduction of an Old Irish Long-beamed plough, made for us by a multi-talented craftsman, Seamus O'Kane of Dungiven, County Derry (Fig. 98). We didn't learn much from growing corn on ridges, as the museum's geese trampled and ate the corn as it ripened, but using the wooden plough confirmed descriptions written around 1800, and made it clear why ploughmen were said to have worked with the plough and its horse team in the way they did.

Some aspects of social relations could be demonstrated in the outdoor museum at Cultra, particularly those connected to the division of labour on farms. The number of vernacular dwellings brought in to the museum meant that women's contribution to farm work was automatically emphasised, especially the processing of farm produce in tasks such as dairying and baking, while the museum's policy of bringing in buildings representing rural crafts, such as blacksmithing, spade making and milling, made it relatively easy to show the tight interconnectedness of the small farming economy. Farmers provided raw materials for rural crafts and industries, and these in turn provided a technical infrastructure necessary to support farming operations, or to process the raw materials produced.

However, there is still a gap between the mechanics of farming displayed in the museum, and curatorial attempts to exhibit key elements of the society supported by this activity, particularly day-to-day social life. We haven't found 'living' interpretative methods such as role-play and drama to have the same authority as the iconic[13] representations achieved by growing crops or living animals. We have tried to deal with social roles and relations in gallery displays, using audio-visual archives, but the gap is still there. Perhaps the nearest we have come to successfully representing social life has been in the celebrations that followed large-scale events, when the country people participating in the event took over and created an experience that seemed to echo a ceilí or harvest home of earlier times.

The Ulster American Folk Park

Like the Ulster Folk and Transport Museum, this is one of the constituent parts of the National Museums Northern Ireland. It began life in 1967 with

99 Liam Corry of the Ulster American Folk Park leading a tour of the Mellon farm, which forms the core of the museum's Irish exhibit buildings.

the explicit aim of celebrating the achievements of the 'Scotch-Irish', Presbyterians who left Ireland in the eighteenth and early nineteenth centuries, but its remit has now been broadened to cover all Irish emigration to America. As at Cultra, most of the exhibits in the outdoor museum displays are buildings brought into the museum from elsewhere; in this case 'elsewhere' includes North America. The American exhibits are displayed in settings that reflect their original sites, and some appropriate farm crops are cultivated, mostly maize and pumpkins. Liam Corry (Fig. 99), who curates the agricultural collections and exhibits, also plants oats and flax in fields beside the Ulster exhibits, and makes lazybeds of potatoes in a 'potato garden'. Liam does not have any staff employed specifically for farming, so livestock are kept to a minimum – a horse, a donkey and some poultry.

The Old World/New World contrasts are one of the most striking aspects of the museum's exhibits. However, its authority is significantly increased by the fact that the Irish exhibits centre on the original Mellon house and farm. The hedges around the nineteenth-century farm fields are now being replanted, and a new lane laid down so that it is possible to 'walk the bounds' of the farm, which Liam hopes can be developed as a nineteenth-century working exhibit. Even in its undeveloped state, a walk along the lane can be used in conjunction with Thomas Mellon's account of his return to the farm on a visit in 1882 as a wonderful contextual guide. Our experience of the walk involved inputs by Liam, and by Brian Lambkin and Paddy Fitzgerald, two senior staff from the Centre for Migration Studies, which is based at the museum. The walk was part of an Autumn School organised by the Centre in 2013. Such a labour-intensive presentation obviously cannot be put on as part of the general visitor experience, but it confirmed the view that person to person communication is the most effective interpretative tool in museum work. The impact of the walking tour is increased both by the beauty of the location, Thomas Mellon's loving, detailed description of it, and the extent to which places mentioned by him are still easily found today.

> When I revisited it in 1882, sixty-four years after I had left it, there was not the slightest correction to be made to my mental map. It was all there in every particular, as I had seen it as a child and still remembered it … The croft, the river brae with its bright spring well under the holly bush, the holm with its beautiful whin and broom … all were in their places as accurately as Camp Hill Cottage itself, with the stable and small orchard beyond the flush.[14]

If the Mellon farm is developed as the staff of the museum hope, it will be both authoritative and enjoyable.

Muckross House and Traditional Farms

Situated in Killarney National Park, Muckross House and Muckross Traditional Farms must be among the most beautifully located historic houses and open-air museums in the world (Fig. 100). The Muckross Estate was gifted to the Irish people in 1932 by the Bourn Vincent family and it became Ireland's very first national park. Although its extensive gardens were open to the public,

Muckross House itself remained closed for three decades following its acquisition by the state. In 1964, a group of local people persuaded the government to allow the House to be opened to the public as a folk museum. It was intended that this facility would place special emphasis on illustrating the traditional way of life of the people of Kerry. The state retained responsibility for the upkeep of Muckross House and gardens. However, a local voluntary body, the Trustees of Muckross House, was formed to manage and develop the museum, its collections and exhibits. In addition, it was always the intention of the Trustees to develop an open-air museum. The decision was taken in the mid-1980s to restore Muckross House to its original state, as a Victorian family mansion. Shortly after, the development of Muckross Traditional Farms commenced on a site adjacent to the House and the folk life material was moved to this new location.

Almost from their inception, the Trustees had established a Research Library, which was responsible for documenting the growing quantity of 'folk' artefacts within the collections. This standard of documentation was a major factor in all three elements within the Muckross complex – the Victorian House, Research Library and Traditional Farms – being awarded fully-accredited museum status, by the Heritage Council, in 2007. Patricia O'Hare, whose post as Research and Educational Officer also includes high-level curatorial and educational work, oversees the documentation of a growing collection of artefacts, books, archival documents and photographs. (A database of 24,000 photographs had been established by 2014.)

Muckross is remarkable in successfully combining commercial initiatives with an ongoing interest in historical accuracy, achieved through scholarly research. Given its situation in the tourist heartland of Ireland, the potential for income generation was recognised very early, and apart from some admission money, the museum has successful craft workshops producing textiles and pottery, along with a smaller book-binding and paper conservation enterprise.

Muckross Traditional Farms represent local farming life in the 1930s and 1940s, the last period when horse-operated machinery was used. Three sizes of farm are represented, small, medium and large, and these are based on actual holdings from the nearby Barleymount area, north-west of Killarney. Farming at all three levels was mixed, producing a range of crops and livestock. Livestock kept on the Traditional Farms include working horses, Kerry cattle, donkeys, pigs, sheep, goats and poultry. Crops grown include potatoes, oats, and hay, and each farmhouse has a well-kept vegetable garden (Fig. 101).

100 The Lower Lake at Killarney, viewed from the terrace of Muckross House.

101 Harrowing with horses at Muckross Traditional Farms, Killarney. (Photo: Toddy Doyle.)

102 Staff and visitors in the schoolhouse exhibit building in the Muckross estate, Killarney.

The Farm Manager, Toddy Doyle, oversees the everyday running of the farms, and has developed a creative programme of activities highlighting special times in the farming year. The annual week-long Féile Chultúir Chiarraí (Festival of Kerry Culture) concentrates on providing a series of hands-on workshops for primary school children each May. This event, which is run in conjunction with Muckross Research Library, has been awarded the Sandford Award for Heritage Education on three separate occasions (2003, 2008, 2013). The Sandford Award is managed by the UK Heritage Education Trust in partnership with Bishop Grosseteste University, Lincoln. In 2003, Muckross was the first site outside of the UK to receive this award. The farms also host many corporate and income-generating events, which make use of the farm buildings and related exhibit buildings, such as a national school house, and the incomparable outdoor setting (Fig. 102).

Down Museum, Downpatrick

Down County Museum is located in an eighteenth-century jail in the centre of Downpatrick. Collections and exhibitions cover aspects of prehistory, the Early Christian and Medieval periods, the Plantation of Ulster and subsequent conflicts, and recent social history and popular culture. Down is one of the few local museums in Ireland to have a significant and coherent collection of farm implements and machinery. The agricultural collection, which was developed under the direction of a former director, Dr Brian Turner, reflects the influence of the charismatic Estyn Evans, the father of Irish folklife studies. In 2014, a permanent gallery was built to house a permanent exhibition on farming and fishing. At the time of writing, two curators, Lesley Simpson and Madeleine McAllister (Fig. 103), had developed the exhibition content and layout, the aim being to display key artefacts related to farming in County Down, and the people who used them. Not surprisingly, County Down-man Harry Ferguson's world-famous tractor is starred, but other distinctively local artefacts are also displayed – a tipping cart, a wooden plough and a wheelless, horse-drawn slipe. One of the most encouraging things about the project is that it is led by the curators. The exhibition's design complements rather than dominates the objects and photographs displayed, and captions are authoritative; different levels of detail are provided in large general panels, individual captions, and detailed flip books. The respect with which the objects are treated affirms the value of the lives of the people who made and used them.

* * *

At a conference once, we confided to a very elegant Oxford don that we feared we might have become cranks. We were studying nineteenth-century field drainage systems and, worryingly, we were finding the subject fascinating! His response was very reassuring. 'But that is the nature of scholarship, and indeed its charm.' We have not worried about becoming odd or obscure ever since. The image of the eccentric antiquarian is charming and an attractive alternative to the stereotype of hard-headed, globally oriented executive that now dominates a lot of Irish professional life. Unfortunately, however, it has become very difficult to maintain a working life based on pottering among esoteric bygones. In the early 1980s, museums throughout Ireland began to respond to state policies, which increasingly emphasised 'performance targets' and 'value for money'. This government-directed push towards quantifiable indicators of performance has been condemned as an example of the 'commodification of culture', but it also has a positive aspect, in that it forced museum staff to put service to the public at the centre of strategic planning. At its best it countered a tendency towards elite mystification within museums, which sometimes provided a front disguising rather mediocre and limited outputs. The need to develop full research and educational programs, and at the same time perform its role as a leisure and tourist amenity, led to scrutiny of display techniques. Some of the results of this scrutiny can be seen in the case studies presented here.

Ways of examining or celebrating the rural past have changed in line with changing stereotypes of country people and rural society in general. In the early twentieth century, when folklife became an academic discipline, scholars in the field were sometimes faced with the contempt of conservative colleagues. Estyn Evans, the father of the subject in the north, recorded that 'In my enquiries into … rural customs and sociology … I got no encouragement from the [Queen's] University [Belfast]. Indeed I faced open hostility from professors who regarded "local studies" as beneath their notice.'[15] Folklife research was a precursor to local studies and the 'people's histories' that have attempted to combat the view that history should only focus on the activities of small, ruling minorities, and special individuals. Evans and his contemporaries deserve praise for their success in getting the new subjects accepted as vital elements in the humanities.

Folklife and folklore approaches to fieldwork and interpretative display have also proved of lasting value. Because many of the 'folk' were illiterate, or had lives not considered important enough to appear in written records, folklife researchers pioneered many of the methods used by researchers in oral history. Because many of the artefacts in folklife collections, such as hand tools used in tillage and harvest, are very simply made from one or two pieces of metal, the ingenuity behind their construction only becomes clear when they are examined in the context of techniques in which they were used. The development of outdoor museums has put such contexts at the centre of interpretation. Presenting an object in relation to others with which it was used, in the building in which it was used, goes a long way towards showing its significance. Outdoor museum exhibits also enable demonstration of many techniques. These demonstrations can be used in education, to entertain general visitors, and sometimes, as outlined above, to further research.

103 Lesley Simpson and Madeleine McAllister of Down County Museum, with exhibits intended for the museum's farming gallery.

However, some aspects of these early approaches had less desirable consequences. As discussed earlier, folklife scholars such as Evans had a poetic vision of the folk, as people mysteriously detached from the ferment of changing human affairs, who lived in age-old harmony with their environment, using local materials and local techniques. When this way of looking at the past underpinned the practical work of rebuilding and furnishing museum exhibit buildings, it could lead to a kind of cultural cleansing, where modern intrusions, such as clocks and ornaments displayed by a dwelling's occupants, might be ruthlessly excluded when the house was rebuilt, and inhabitants' attempts to improve their living space, for example, by covering the beams and interior thatch with wooden boards, or even sacking, were removed, along with rooms and partitions which were sometimes added when a family could afford them. The removal of these impure elements parallels the search for Gaelic purity by cultural revivalists, lampooned in Flann O'Brien's great book *An Béal Bocht* (The Poor Mouth).

> There was a man in this townland at the time and he was named Sitric O'Sanassa … The gentlemen from Dublin … praised him for his Gaelic poverty and stated that they never saw anyone who appeared so truly Gaelic. One of the gentlemen broke a little bottle of water which Sitric had, because, said he, it spoiled the effect.[16]

Diarmuid Ó Giolláin has pointed out that isolation and poverty were seen as essential to the notion of unspoilt tradition, as prosperity and integration would automatically mean contact with polluting modern values.[17]

Another aspect of early theory that has become problematic in the way it has shaped museum displays is the view of the unchanging nature of folk tradition. As discussed above, this way of looking at rural life now seems far-fetched in the manner that it could dismiss huge historical changes as irrelevant to underlying and ancient cultural and even psychological traits. In one paper, for example, Estyn Evans suggested that Charles Darwin's independent brain and character (and beetling brow) might be genetically inherited from the Beaker folk who lived in the Welsh Borders in the Third Millennium BC, an area which Evans also paradoxically identifies as crucial to the world-changing industrial revolution.[18]

In a museum context, the exhibit buildings produced by this underplaying (or denial) of change can seem very attractive to people who value the aesthetic wholeness produced by the use of local materials and techniques, but an unintended consequence can be that it presents a model of society that is labeled 'functionalist' by social scientists; a theoretical approach that presents society as a well-oiled machine, where change is gradual, and conflict is uncommon and short-term, a model that seems very unsuited to deepening understanding of, for example, Northern Ireland's religious/political/ethnic divisions.

It is a model, also, that does not engage easily with changing perceptions of what rural people are like. Many urban people interested in rural issues, especially those related to care of the environment, methods of livestock management, and concerns about methods of food production, far from seeing country people as sensitive 'tradition bearers', have an equally distorted view, which sees them as ruthless despoilers.

Museum displays can, and should, have relevance to both negative and positive models that people have of the rural past. Pollution, over-cropping, and over-reliance on chemicals are not new problems, but have been recorded and discussed in Ireland for at least three centuries. The holistic approach developed in early folk museums – displaying the interconnectedness of rural life – is well-suited to showing the knock-on effects of actions that originally seemed discretely self-contained. Folk museums and heritage centres, especially those with outdoor exhibits, can use iconic representations (objects and activities that participate in the reality that they represent, for example, a field of grain or a Kerry cow) to deepen understanding of past mistakes and disasters, and also to demonstrate the brilliance and ingenuity of people who survived against all the odds, and even found the resource to express themselves in music, poetry and visual arts that still speak to us directly today.

Conclusion

THIS OUTLINE OF FARMING HISTORY has been arbitrarily selective, and pushed by an ideological agenda: to celebrate the technical, social and cultural achievements of Irish farmers and farming society. Despite the brutality and stupidity of individuals and groups at all social levels, and the misery they inflicted, the history of Irish farming is a success story; how big a commercial success became starkly clear in the recent economic crash, when agriculture was one part of the Irish economy that still generated profits of billions of euros.

Kerr's Ass

We borrowed the loan of Kerr's big ass
To go to Dundalk with butter,
Brought him home the evening before the market
An exile that night in Mucker.

We heeled up the cart before the door,
We took the harness inside –
The straw-stuffed straddle, the broken breeching
With bits of bull-wire tied;

The winkers that had no choke-band,
The collar and the reins …
In Ealing Broadway, London Town,
I name their several names

Until a world comes to life –
Morning, the silent bog,
And the god of imagination waking
In a Mucker fog.

Patrick Kavanagh[1]

104 A blacksmith trimming a donkey's hooves. (Photo: National Museums Northern Ireland.)

The social structures of Irish rural society have been impoverished as well as enriched by the huge political, economic and technical changes of the last three centuries. If we understand communities to be created and maintained by close kinship and neighbourly ties, continually maintained and strengthened by face-to-face interaction and shared working arrangements, there is little doubt that community life in rural Ireland has been greatly weakened by depopulation, farm consolidation and mechanisation. However, the sense of belonging that comes from an awareness of a shared heritage, symbolically re-affirmed in festivals and other heritage products, is alive and well. 'Globalisation' often obliterates the local, but it can also make us aware of the value of local achievements and the importance of remembering and celebrating them (Fig. 104).

Notes

PREFACE

1 Iris Murdoch, *The Red and the Green* (New York: Avon Books, 1965), p. 183.

2 Brendan Behan, *Borstal Boy* (London: Corgi Books, 1958 [1980]), p. 290.

CHAPTER 1
Country people talking

1 Arthur Young, *A Tour in Ireland*, 2 vols (London, 1780), vol. 2, part 1, p. 457.

2 John Millington Synge, *The Playboy of the Western World* (Oxford: Oxford University Press, 1998), Act 1, Scene 1.

3 John E. Messenger, lecture, Queen's University of Belfast, 1968.

4 Quentin Crisp, *The Naked Civil Servant* (London: Flamingo, 1968 [1985]), p. 53.

5 Jonathan Bell, *Ulster Farming Families, 1930–1960* (Belfast: Ulster Historical Foundation, 2005), p. 8.

6 John Hewitt, 'Country Speech' from *The Day of the Corncrake: Poems of the Nine Glens* (Belfast: Glens of Antrim Historical Society, 1969), p. 14.

7 Samuel Beckett, *Malone Dies* (London: Penguin, 1951 [1971]), p. 38.

8 Gaynor Kavanagh, *Dream Spaces: Memory and the Museum* (London: University of Leicester Press, 2000), p. 11.

9 Eric Hobsbawm, *On History* (London: Weidenfeld & Nicolson, 1997), p. 206.

10 Kavanagh, *Dream Spaces*, p. 19.

CHAPTER 2
The family

1 John Berger, *Pig Earth* (London: Writers and Readers Publishing Co-operative, 1979), p. 96.

2 Conrad M. Arensberg and Solon T. Kimball, *Family and Community in Ireland*, 2nd ed. (Cambridge, MA: Harvard University Press, 1940 [1968]), pp 56–8.

3 Conrad M. Arensberg, *The Irish Countryman: An Anthropological Study* (London: MacMillan, 1937), p. 73.

4 John E. Messenger, '*Man of Aran* Revisited', *University Review*, 3:9 (Dublin, 1963), p. 25.

5 Ibid., p. 29.

6 Jonathan Bell, 'Economic Change in the Dunfanaghy Area of North Donegal, 1900–1940' (PhD, Queen's University Belfast, 1982), pp 83–5. Eileen Kane, 'The Changing Role of the Family in a Rural Irish Community', *Journal of Comparative Family Studies*, 10:2 (1979), pp 142–62.

7 Damian Hannan, *Displacement and Development: Class, Kinship and Social Change in Irish Rural Communities* (Dublin: Economic and Social Research Institute, 1979), p. 7.

8 Paul M. Sacks, *The Donegal Mafia: An Irish Political Machine* (New Haven: Yale University Press, 1976), p. 42.

9 John McGahern, *The Dark* (London: Faber & Faber, 1965), p. 27.

10 Ibid., pp 147–8.

11 F.R. Higgins, 'Father and Son' from Brendan Kennelly (ed.), *The Penguin Book of Irish Verse* (London: Penguin, 1970), p. 330.

12 Rosemary Harris, *Prejudice and Tolerance in Ulster* (Manchester: Manchester University Press, 1972), p. 5.

13 C. Olcott, E.K. Ball, R.J. Young, 'Mother Machree' (1910).

14 'Gentle Mother' (traditional, arranged Tony Allen).

15 Betty Sue Perry, 'Medals for Mothers' (Nashville: Sure Fire Music Inc., 1969).

16 Arensberg and Kimball, *Family and Community in Ireland*, p. 58.

17 Patrick Kavanagh, 'Tarry Flynn 111' from *Collected Poems* (London: Martin, Brian & O'Keeffe, 1964 [1972]), p. 37.

18 This way of looking at marriage is particularly clear in structuralist theory. 'Both the exchange of women and the exchange of food are means of securing or of displaying the interlocking of social groups with one another.' Claude Lévi-Strauss, *The Savage Mind* (London: Weidenfeld and Nicolson, 1966 [1972]), p. 109.

19 Katherine Tynan, *Peeps at Many Lands: Ireland* (London: Black, 1909).

20 Sophie Gallagher, 'Women Rule the Plough … Even in 1957' Boyletm.com/tm/sophie-gallagher.

21 S.J. Connolly, 'Marriage' in Connolly (ed.), *The Oxford Companion to Irish History* (Oxford: Oxford University Press, 1998), p. 350.

22 Mary Carberry, *The Farm by Lough Gur* (Cork: Mercier Press, 1937 [1973]), p. 46. John E. Messenger, '*Man of Aran* Revisited' *University Review*, 3:9 (Dublin, 1963), p. 24.

23 Kevin Danaher, *In Ireland Long Ago* (Cork: Mercier Press, 1962 [1969]), p. 157.

24 Claudia Kinmouth, *Irish Rural Interiors* (New Haven: Yale, 2006), pp 160–2.

25 Caoimhín Ó Danachair, quoted in Kinmouth, *Irish Rural Interiors*, p. 154.

26 Percy French, 'They're Cuttin' the Corn in Creeslough Today'.

27 Traditional, 'Mick Maguire'.

28 Peig Sayers, *Peig* (Dublin: Comhlacht Oideachais n hÉireann, 1936 [1969]), pp 123–4.

29 Peig Sayers, *The Autobiography of Peig Sayers* (trans. Bryan MacMahon) (Syracuse NY: Syracuse University Press, 1974), pp 150–2.

30 Ulster Folk and Transport Museum Archive, unclassified.

31 William Trevor, 'The Ballroom of Romance' from *The Ballroom of Romance and Other Stories* (London: Bodley Head, 1972).

32 Asenath Nicholson, *Ireland's Welcome to the Stranger* (Dublin: Lilliput Press, 2002), pp 67–8.

33 W.F. Marshall, 'Me and Me Da' from *Livin' in Drumlister* (Dundonald: Blackstaff, 1983).

34 S.J. Connolly, 'Marriage', p. 350.

35 Carmel Kelleher and Ann O'Mahony, *Marginalisation in Irish Agriculture* (Dublin: An Foras Talúntas, 1984), pp 27–8.

36 Brody, *Inishkillane*, p. 98.

37 Ibid., p. 100.

38 Irish Farmers' Association, *People and the Land* (Dublin: IFA, 1972), p. 11.

39 Brody, *Inishkillane*, p. 42.

40 Joanna Bourke, *Husbandry to Housewifery: Women, Economic Change, and Housework in Ireland, 1890–1914* (Oxford: Clarendon Press, 1993), p. 149.

41 Jonathan Bell, *Ulster Farming Families* (Belfast: Ulster Historical Foundation, 2005), p. 43.

42 Harris, *Prejudice and Tolerance in Ulster*, pp 61–4.

43 Bell, *Ulster Farming Families*, pp 45–6.

44 Carberry, *The Farm by Lough Gur*, p. 12.

45 Ibid., p. 9.

46 Lapping hay was particularly associated with the northern half of Ireland. It was very labour-intensive, involving making each armful of hay into a hollow roll. Rain ran off the roll, while the hollow in its centre allowed air to circulate through the hay, speeding up drying. Lapping was one of the few 'common' Irish farming techniques praised by nineteenth-century agriculturalists.

47 Bell, *Ulster Farming Families*, p. 51.

48 We are grateful to Robbie Hannan for the following, taken from the Royal Irish Academy, *Dictionary of the Irish Language*. 'A compound of ben + trebthach "woman + householder, farmer"; treb(th)achas is given as householding, cultivating, ploughing. It is possible that by necessity that a baintreach was a woman who ploughs; a stricter etymology might be 'woman householder, farmer'.

49 Jonathan Bell and Mervyn Watson, *Farming in North and East County Down: An Oral History* (Downpatrick: Down County Museum, 2011), p. 44.

50 The allocation of prizes became more prescriptive, however. In 1956, at Nenagh in County Tipperary, a new 'marriage

incentive' was introduced. The 'Queen of the Plough' would be given £100 if under 25 years of age, on her wedding morning. www.npa.ie/ploughing/history-of-the-npa-championship.

51 Mervyn Watson 'Standardisation of Pig Production: the Case of the Large White Ulster Pig', *Ulster Folklife*, 34 (1988), pp 1–15.

52 W.L. Micks, *An Acount of the … Congested Districts Board for Ireland from 1891 to 1923* (Dublin: Eason, 1925).

53 Jonathan Bell and Mervyn Watson, *A History of Irish Farming* (Dublin: Four Courts Press, 2008), pp 246–7.

54 Liam Downey, 'The Cork Butter Exchange', *Ulster Folklife*, 57 (2014), pp 38–48.

55 Bourke, *Husbandry to Housewifery*, p. 85.

56 Bell and Watson, *A History of Irish Farming*, pp 246–7.

57 Harris, *Prejudice and Tolerance in Ulster*, p. 5.

58 Bourke, *Husbandry to Housewifery*, p. 171.

59 Bell, *Ulster Farming Families*, p. 53.

60 Bourke, *Husbandry to Housewifery*, p. 188.

61 Damian Hannan, *Rural Exodus* (London: Chapman, 1970), p. 23.

62 Ibid., p. 107.

63 Carberry, *The Farm by Lough Gur*, p. 47.

64 Hannan, *Rural Exodus*, pp 11 and 23.

65 Bell and Watson, *A History of Irish Farming*, p. 45.

66 T.M. Charles-Edwards et al., 'Agriculture' in Connolly (ed.), *Oxford Companion to Irish History*, pp 6–10.

67 Joe Barry, 'Farm Mechanisation' in Brian Lalor (ed.), *The Encyclopaedia of Ireland* (Dublin: Gill & Macmillan, 2003), p. 376. Bell and Watson, *A History of Irish Farming*, pp 291–3.

68 Eric Donald, 'Agribusiness' in Brian Lalor (ed.), *The Encyclopaedia of Ireland* (Dublin: Gill & Macmillan, 2003), p. 11.

CHAPTER 3
The neighbours

1 Karl Marx and Friedrich Engels, *The Communist Manifesto* (Fairford: Echo Library, 1848 [2009]), p. 9.

2 Karl Marx, 'The Eighteenth Brumaire of Louis Bonaparte' in Karl Marx and Frederick Engels, *Selected Works* (London: Lawrence and Wishart (1968 [1980])), pp 170–1.

3 Anne O'Dowd, *Meitheal: A Study of Co-operative Labour in Rural Ireland*. Common terms for exchange of help between groups of neighbouring farmers: meitheal; cruinniú; boon; banville; camp; gathering; fiddler. (Comhairle Bhéaloideas Éireann: Dublin, 1981), pp 39–66. Common terms for exchange of help between two neighbouring farmers: comhar; morrowing; cosnet; joining; swapping; working in means.

4 Types of work done: spadework; ploughing; planting (potatoes, corn etc.); turf cutting; digging potatoes; pulling flax; hay making; cutting and binding corn; making hay and corn stacks; carting hay and corn; threshing grain with flails; help with portable threshing machine; winnowing; making kelp; sheep shearing; pig killing; thatching; fencing; building; spinning; quilting; beetling and scutching flax; embroidery. O'Dowd, *Meitheal*, pp 77–9.

5 Bell, 'Economic Change in the Dunfanaghy Area of North Donegal', p. 106.

6 Robbie Hannan and Jonathan Bell, 'The Bothóg' in Trefor M. Owen (ed.), *From Corrib to Cultra* (Holywood: Ulster Folk and Transport Museum, 2000), pp 71–8.

7 Conrad M. Arensberg, *The Irish Countryman: An Anthropological Study* (London: MacMillan, 1937), pp 68–9.

8 Ibid.

9 R. Thompson, *Statistical Survey of the County of Meath, 1802*, quoted in O'Dowd, *Meitheal*, p. 32.

10 Jonathan Bell, *Ulster Farming Families*, p. 61.

11 Bell, 'Economic Change in Dunfanaghy', p. 103.

12 Bell and Watson, *A History of Irish Farming*, p. 77.

13 Bell, *Ulster Farming Families*, p. 68.

14 Bell, 'Economic Change in Dunfanaghy', p. 101.

15 O'Dowd, *Meitheal*, p. 75.

16 Bell, 'Economic Change in Dunfanaghy', p. 69.

17 Ibid., p. 63.

18 Columcille, Granard, Longford, 1955: O'Dowd, *Meitheal*, pp 84–5.

19 Ibid., p. 85.

20 Arensberg and Kimball, *Family and Community in Ireland*, pp 71–2.

21 Peter Gibbon, 'Arensberg and Kimball Reevisited', *Economy and Society*, 2:4 (1973), pp 486–7.

22 Bell, *Ulster Farming Families*, pp 58–5.

23 O'Dowd, *Meitheal*, pp 33–4.

24 Bell, *Ulster Farming Families*, pp 67–8.

25 O'Dowd, *Meitheal*, p. 89.

26 Bell, *Ulster Farming Families*, pp 67–8.

27 Ibid.

28 O'Dowd, *Meitheal*, p. 74.

29 Ibid., pp 113–18.

30 Bell, *Ulster Farming Families*, p. 69.

31 Arensberg, *The Irish Countryman*, p. 113.

32 Bell and Watson, *Farming in North and East County Down*, p. 52.

33 Brody, *Inishkillane*, p. 14.

34 Bell and Watson, *Farming in North and East County Down,* p. 51.

35 Ibid., p. 52.

36 Patrick Bolger, *The Irish Co-operative Movement* (Dublin: IAOS, 1977), p. 249.

37 Sinn Féin, *Eire Nua: The Social and Economic Programme of Sinn Féin* (Dublin: Sinn Féin, 1971), p. 4.

38 Bolger, *The Irish Co-operative Movement*, p. 108.

39 M. Digby, *The World Co-operative Movement* (London: Hutchinson, 1948), p. 10.

40 Irish Farmers' Association, *People and the Land* (Dublin: Irish Farmers' Association, 1972), pp 28–9.

41 Ibid., p. 30.

42 Agri-Food Strategy Board, *Going for Growth: A Strategic Action Plan in Support of the Northern Ireland Agri-Food Industry* (Belfast, 2013), pp 28, 30.

43 Patrick Kavanagh, *Collected Poems* (London: Martin Brian and O'Keefe, 1972 [1973]), pp 28–9.

CHAPTER 4
Farm labourers and servants

1 David Fitzpatrick, 'The Disappearance of the Irish Agricultural Labourer', *Irish Economic and Social History*, 7 (Dublin, 1980), pp 66–92.

2 Jonathan Bell and Mervyn Watson, *Rooted in the Soil: A History of Cottage Gardens and Allotments in Ireland since 1750* (Dublin: Four Courts Press, 2012), pp 15–21.

3 S.J. Connolly, 'Cottier' in Connolly (ed.), *The Oxford Companion to Irish History*, p. 126.

4 Oliver MacDonagh, 'The Economy and Society 1830–45' in W.E. Vaughan (ed.), *A New History of Ireland*, v (Oxford: Clarendon Press, 1989), p. 218.

5 Young, *A Tour in Ireland*, vol. 2, pp 109–11.

6 Ibid., p. 111.

7 Kevin O'Neill, *Family and Farm in Pre-Famine Ireland* (Madison, WI: University Press, 1984), p. 104.

8 Young, *A Tour in Ireland*, vol. 2, pp 112–13.

9 Ibid., p. 25.

10 Robert Beatson, 'On Cottages', *The Irish Agricultural Magazine* (Dublin, 1793), p. 139.

11 John Forbes, *Memorandums made in Ireland in the Autumn of 1852*, vol. 2 (London: Smith, Elder and Co., 1853), pp 375–6.

12 Cormac Ó Gráda, 'Poverty, Population and Agriculture, 1801–45' in Vaughan (ed.), *A New History of Ireland*, v, p. 127.

13 S.J. Connolly, 'Seasonal Migration' in Connolly (ed.), *The Oxford Companion to Irish History*, p. 504.

14 Ibid.

15 Anne O'Dowd, *Spalpeens and Tattie Hokers* (Dublin: Irish Academic Press, 1991), p. 28.

16 W.L. Micks, *An Account of the … Congested Districts Board for Ireland, from 1891 to 1923* (Dublin: Eason & Sons, 1925), p. 245.

17 Ruth-Ann Harris, 'Migratory Labour' in Lalor (ed.), *The Encyclopaedia of Ireland*, p. 724.

18 J.E. Handley, *The Irish in Modern Scotland* (Cork: Cork University Press, 1947), p. 171.

19 David Fitzpatrick, 'A Peculiar Tramping People' in Vaughan, *A New History of Ireland*, v, p. 631.

20 O'Dowd, *Spalpeens and Tattie Hokers*, p. 125.

21 Parliamentary Commission on Labour, 1893, quoted in O'Dowd, *Spalpeens and Tattie Hokers*, p. 31.

22 Daniel Corkery, *The Hidden Ireland* (Dublin: Gill & Macmillan, 1924 [1973]), p. 192.

23 O'Dowd, *Spalpeens and Tattie Hokers*, p. 10.

24 An tAthair Padraig Ua Duinnín, *Amhráin Eoghan Ruaidh Uí Súilleabháin* (Gaelic League: Dublin, 1901), p. 53.

25 Fitzpatrick, 'A Peculiar Tramping People', p. 631.

26 Micks, *An Account of the … Congested Districts Board for Ireland from 1891 to 1923*, p. 243.

27 Inventory of William Stevenson, Legecory, County Armagh, 1717. Public Records Office of Northern Ireland, T1062/18.

28 W.S. Mason, *An Account of Ireland, Statistical and Political*, vol. 1 (London, 1814), p. 125.

29 O'Dowd, *Spalpeens and Tattie Hokers*, p. 104.

30 Bell, *Ulster Farming Families*, p. 80.

31 *The Dungannon News*, 15 November 1894.

32 O'Dowd, *Spalpeens and Tattie Hokers*, pp 301–5. Jonathan Bell, 'Hiring Fairs in Ulster', *Ulster Folklife*, 25 (1979), p. 76.

33 Seán Beattie, 'The Hiring Fair System in Donegal' in Jim McLaughlin and Seán Beattie (eds), *Atlas of County Donegal* (Cork: Cork University Press, 2013), p. 256.

34 Patrick MacGill, *Children of the Dead End* (Ascot: Caliban Books, 1914 [1970]), p. 30.

35 Ibid., pp 30–2.

36 Bell, 'Hiring Fairs in Ulster', p. 70.

37 MacGill, *Children of the Dead End*, p. 231

38 Bell, *Ulster Farming Families*, p. 80.

39 Bell, 'Hiring Fairs in Ulster', p. 71.

40 O'Dowd, *Spalpeens and Tattie Hokers*, p. 134.

41 Bell, 'Hiring Fairs in Ulster', p. 71.

42 Ibid., p. 72.

43 MacGill, *Children of the Dead End*, pp 35–6.

44 Ibid., p. 58.

45 This applied to farm workers of all kinds. O'Dowd, *Spalpeens and Tattie Hokers*, pp 135–9.

46 Bell, *Ulster Farming Families*, p. 82.

47 Beattie, 'The Hiring Fair System in Donegal', p. 258.

48 Ministry of Agriculture for Northern Ireland, *The Conditions of Employment of Agricultural Workers in Northern Ireland* (Belfast: HMSO, 1938), p. 92.

49 Anon., 'Derry Hiring Fair' in May Blair, *Hiring Fairs and Market Places* (Belfast: Appletree Press, 2007).

50 John Clifford, 'Larne Hiring Fair' in *Poems of John Clifford* (Larne: Larne and District Folklore Society, 1984).

51 MacGill, *Children of the Dead End*, p. 33.

52 Liam MacGabhann, 'The Magic of the Isles' from *Rags, Robes and Rebels* (Dublin: Eibhlinn Press, 1939), p. 38. Quoted in O'Dowd, *Spalpeens and Tattie Hokers*, pp 176 and 406.

53 Heather Holmes, *Tattie Howkers: Irish Potato Workers in Ayrshire* (Ayr: Ayrshire Archaeological and Natural History Society, 2005), p. 11.

54 Holmes, *Tattie Howkers*, p. 51.

55 Ibid., p. 34.

56 Ibid., pp 30 and 37.

57 Ibid., p. 39.

58 MacGill, *Children of the Dead End*, pp 74–5.

59 M.G. Wallace, 'The Earnings of Irish Migratory Labourers in England and Scotland, Season 1904', Department of Agriculture and Technical Instruction for Ireland, *Journal* (Dublin, 1905), p. 448.

60 Holmes, *Tattie Howkers*, p. 87.

61 Anton McNulty, 'A Tragedy Recalled', *Mayo News*, 11 September 2007

62 Peadar O'Donnell, 'The Irish Labour Movement: the Scottish Dimension'. Lecture given at a conference organised by the Irish Labour History Society in 1981.

63 Holmes, *Tattie Howkers*, pp 89–99.

64 Wallace, 'Earnings of Irish Migratory Labourers in England and Scotland', p. 561.

65 Fitzpatrick, 'A Peculiar Tramping People', p. 630.

66 Bell, *Ulster Farming Families*, p. 89.

67 Bell, 'Economic Change in the Dunfanaghy Area of North Donegal', p. 161.

68 O'Dowd, *Spalpeens and Tattie Hokers*, pp 134–5.

69 Carbery, *The Farm by Lough Gur*, pp 1, 4, 21, 22, 37, 38, 49, 59.

70 Ibid., p. 24.

71 Ibid., p. 16.

72 Bell, 'Economic Change in the Dunfanaghy Area of North Donegal', pp 134–5.

73 O'Dowd, *Spalpeens and Tattie Hokers*, p. 10.

74 Ibid., pp 268–9.

75 Ibid., p. 270.

76 Holmes, *Tattie Howkers*, pp 123–5.

77 Peadar O'Donnell, 'The Irish Labour Movement; The Scottish Dimension'.

78 James S. Donnelly Jr, 'Pastorini and Captain Rock: Millenarianism and Sectarianism in the Rockite Movement 1821–1824' in S. Clark and James S. Donnelly Jr (eds), *Irish Peasants: Violence and Unrest* (Madison: University of Wisconsin, 1983), pp 102–42.

79 Bell and Watson, *A History of Irish Farming*, pp 104–5.

80 J.W. Boyle, 'A Marginal Figure: the Irish Rural Labourer' in Clarke and Donnelly (eds), *Irish Peasants*, p. 316.

81 Bell and Watson, *A History of Irish Farming*, p. 188.

82 Boyle, 'A Marginal Figure: the Irish Rural Labourer', p. 317

83 Ibid., p. 328.

84 Holmes, *Tattie Howkers*, pp 121–3.

85 Ibid., p. 124.

86 Eugene Coyle, 'Larkinism and the 1913 County Dublin Farm Labourers' Dispute, 1913', *Dublin Historical Record*, 58:2 (Autumn, 2005), pp 176–90.

87 Larkin's attitude to farm labourers was not always uncritical. In 1941, he suggested that farm workers who had been given small holdings should be evicted if they did not improve them, a position sometimes used to justify the murder of a landlord, Lord Leitrim, in the nineteenth century.

88 Boyle, 'A Marginal Figure: the Irish Rural Labourer', p. 325.

89 Ibid., p. 324.

90 Fitzpatrick, 'The Disappearance of the Irish Agricultural Labourer', p. 80.

91 Department of Agriculture and Technical Instruction for Ireland, *Journal* (Dublin: HMSO, 1918), pp 319–20.

92 Ibid.

93 Department of Agriculture and Technical Instruction for Ireland, *Journal* (Dublin: HMSO, 1922), p. 118.

94 Fitzpatrick, 'The Disappearance of the Irish Agricultural Labourer', p. 66.

95 Boyle, 'A Marginal Figure: the Irish Rural Labourer', p. 334. Fitzpatrick, 'The Disappearance of the Irish Agricultural Labourer'.

96 Ibid., p. 74.

CHAPTER 5
A sense of belonging

1 John Hewitt, 'Sunset over Glenaan' from *The Day of the Corncrake* (Belfast: Glens of Antrim Historical Society, 1984), p. 15.

2 E.E. Evans, *The Personality of Ireland* (Cambridge: Cambridge University Press, 1973 [1992]), pp xi, 66.

3 L.P. Curtis, *Apes and Angels* (London: Smithsonian Institute, 1997).

4 Seán Ó Faolain, 'Magical Ireland' in Cyril Moore, *Countrygoer: Introducing Ireland* (London, 1947), pp 4–9.

5 Bell and Watson, *A History of Irish Farming*, p. 234.

6 Royal Dublin Society, Proceedings, 126 (Dublin, 1890), quoted in Patrick Leonard Curran, *Kerry and Dexter Cattle, and Other Irish Breeds* (Dublin: Royal Dublin Society, 1990), p. 55.

7 The Farmer and Stockbreeder, *Britain Can Breed It*, ed. J.P. Goodwin (1949), quoted in Curran, *Kerry and Dexter Cattle*, p. 55.

8 Mervyn Watson, 'Irish Moiled Cattle', *Ulster Folklife*, 36 (1990).

9 Jonathan Bell, 'Last Sheaves, Ancient Cattle and Protestant Bibles', *Bealóideas* (1985).

10 A.T.Q. Stewart, *The Shape of Irish History* (Belfast: McGill-Queen's University Press, 2001).

11 John Berger has argued that European peasants in general tend to idealise the past as a time when each farming family was free to struggle against scarcity without outside interference. Berger, *Pig Earth*, p. 201.

12 Siamsa Tíre, *Publicity brochure* (Finuge, 1971).

13 Hobsbawm quoted in Gerard Delanty, *Community* (London: Routledge, 2003), p. v.

14 Delanty, *Community*, pp 14–33.

15 Ibid., pp 33, 186.

16 Lorna Sage, *Bad Blood* (London: Fourth Estate, 2001), pp 134–5.

17 Thomas M. Wilson and Hastings Donnan, *The Anthropology of Ireland* (Oxford, Berg, 2006), p. 165.

18 S.L. Popkin, 'The Rational Peasant', *Theory and Society*, 9:3 (1980), pp 411–20.

19 Delanty, *Community*, p. 2.

20 E.P. Thompson, *The Making of the English Working Class* (London: Penguin, 1963 [1980]), p. 255.

21 John Messenger, *Inis Beag, Isle of Ireland* (New York: Holt, Rinehart and Winston, 1969), pp 4–5.

22 John E. Messenger, lectures, Queen's University Belfast, 1968.

23 John E. Messenger, '*Man of Aran* Revisited', *University Review*, 3:9 (Dublin, 1963), pp 15–47.

24 Paul Henry, *An Irish Portrait: the Autobiography of Paul Henry* (London: Batsford, 1952), p. 208.

25 Brody, *Inishkillane*, pp 92, 120, 126.

26 Bourke, *Husbandry and Housewifery*, pp 37–8.

27 Edna O'Brien, *The Country Girls* (London: Penguin [1960], 1987), p. 132.

28 Genesis 8:22 (King James version).

29 Hewitt, 'Sunset over Glenann'.

CHAPTER 6
Horse ploughing matches: history and heritage

1 *Irish News* (Belfast), 12 February 1991, p. 5.

2 Mervyn Watson, 'Backins, Hintins, Ins and Outs and Turnouts: a Study of Horse Ploughing Societies in Northern Ireland' (MA, Queen's University Belfast, 1991), p. 31.

3 *Irish Farmers' Journal and Weekly Intelligencer*, vol. 5; 'Ploughing Match' (Dublin, 1817), p. 167.

4 *Irish Farmers' Journal and Weekly Intelligencer*, 'Report on ploughing trials' (Dublin, 1813), p. 10.

5 *Irish Farmers' Gazette* (Dublin, 1846), p. 763.

6 *Irish Farmers' Journal and Weekly Intelligencer*, 5, p. 283.

7 *The Quarterly Journal of Agriculture*, 4; W. Blackwood & T. Caldwell, 'On the objects and effects of the late Farming Society of Ireland' (Edinburgh & London, 1834), p. 511.

8 *Irish Farmer's Journal and Weekly Intelligencer*, 5, p. 335.

9 *The Quarterly Journal of Agriculture*, 4, pp 513–14.

10 Ibid., p. 514.

11 *Irish Farmers' Journal and Weekly Intelligencer*, 5, 'Ploughs', p. 167.

12 *The Quarterly Journal of Agriculture*, 4, p. 525.

13 *Irish Farmers' Journal and Weekly Intelligencer*, 5, 'Kilkenny District Ploughing Match', p. 225.

14 Ibid.

15 *Irish Farmers' Journal and Weekly Intelligencer* (Dublin, 1820), p. 241.

16 *Irish Farmers' Journal and Weekly Intelligencer*, 5, 'Kilkenny District Ploughing Match', p. 225.

17 *The Quarterly Journal of Agriculture*, 4, p. 525.

18 *Irish Farmers' Journal and Weekly Intelligencer*, 5, 'Kilkenny District Ploughing Match', p. 225.

19 *Irish Farmers' Journal and Weekly Intelligencer*, 5, 'Ploughing Match', p. 167.

20 Victor Turner, *The Forest of Symbols* (Ithaca, NY: Cornell University Press, 1967), p. 28.

21 J.J. Bergin, *Song of the Plough*, archiver.rootsweb.ancestry.com/IrelandGen Web/2009–06/1244812741.

22 During the nineteenth century the two main types of improved plough that were widely used in Ireland were the Scottish swing plough and the English wheel plough. These can still be seen at horse ploughing matches today.

23 Bunreacht na hÉireann, 29 December 1937.

24 *Weekly Irish Times*, 8 February 1939.

25 *Weekly Irish Times*, 18 February 1939.

26 *Ci News The Webportal for Christians*, www.cinews.ie/article.php?articl=10855.

27 Watson, 'Backins, hintins, ins and outs and turnouts', p. 31.

28 Diarmuid Ó Giolláin, 'Perspectives in the Study of Folk-Religion', *Ulster Folklife*, 36 (1990), pp 66–73.

29 www.npa.ie, History of the NPA & Championships, p. 2.

30 *Weekly Irish Times*, 21 February 1931.

31 Ibid.

32 Ibid.

33 Victor Turner, *A Celebration of Ritual* (Washington DC: Smithsonian Institution, 1982), p. 28.

34 A.P. Cohen, *The Symbolic Construction of Community* (London: Ellis Horwood Ltd, Chichester and Tavistock Publications, 1985), p. 50.

35 Mary E. Daly, *The First Department: a History of the Department of Agriculture* (Dublin: Institute of Public Administration, 2002), p. 182.

36 Ibid., p. 184.

37 Bryce Evans, 'Notorious Anarchists? The Irish Smallholder and the State during the Emergency, 1939–45' in William Sheehan and Maura Cronin (eds), *Riotous Assemblies: Rebels, Riots & Revolts* (Cork: Mercier Press, 2011) p. 193.

38 National Ploughing Association, p. 4.

39 *Weekly Irish Times*, 25 February 1933, p. 6.

40 Ibid.

41 Ibid.

42 Watson, 'Backins, Hintins, Ins and Outs and Turnouts', p. 13.

43 Ibid., p. 14.

44 *Belfast Newsletter*, 17 February 1938.

45 Ibid.

46 Daly, *The First Department*, pp 185–6.

47 Ibid., p. 224.

48 Department of Agriculture and Technical Instruction, *Journal*, vols 41–2, p. 174.

49 Department of Agriculture Ireland. *Annual Report 1942*, p. 149.

50 Bryce Evans, 'Notorious Anarchists', p. 197.

51 Ibid.

52 Ibid., pp 195–7, 199, 201.

53 Ibid., pp 198, 201, 202, 204, 206.

54 Ibid., p. 207.

55 Daly, *The First Department*, p. 224.

56 J.J. Bergin, *Song of the Plough*, archiver.rootsweb.ancestry.com

57 Dáil Éireann, vol. 89; 4 March 1943, 'Private Deputies' Business'.

58 www.npa.ie, p. 3.

59 Cohen, *The Symbolic Construction of Community*, p. 99.

60 Bryce Evans, 'Notorious Anarchists?', p. 191.

61 *Irish Times*, 22 February 1941.

62 *Irish Times*, 5 March 1943.

63 Dáil Éireann, vol. 89; 4 March 1943, 'Private Deputies' Business'.

64 www.abbeydorneyploughingsociety.com.

65 Watson, 'Backins, Hintins, Ins and Outs and Turnouts', p. 25.

66 *Belfast Newsletter*, 18 February 1923

67 Watson, 'Backins, Hintins, Ins and Outs and Turnouts', p. 25.

68 Ibid., p. 28.

69 Mervyn Watson, 'The Role of the Horse on Irish Farms' in Trefor M. Owen (ed.), *From Corrib to Cultra* (Belfast: Institute of Irish Studies, Queen's University Belfast in association with the Ulster Folk and Transport Museum, 2000), p. 134.

70 www.abbeydorneyploughingsociety.com.

71 Watson, 'Backins, Hintins, Ins and Outs and Turnouts', p. 51.

72 Mervyn Watson, 'The Role of the Horse on Irish Farms', p. 134.

73 Watson, 'Backins, Hintins, Ins and Outs and Turnouts', p. 35.

74 Ibid., pp 34–5.

75 Ibid., p. 35.

76 www.independent.ie, 'Kings of the Wee County', 25 September 2007.

77 Watson, 'Backins, Hintins, Ins and Outs and Turnouts', p. 36.

78 www.southernstar.ie, 'Ploughing Back on Track Again at Cahermore', 14 February 2009.

79 www.npa.ie, 2013 Results Under-40 Horse Class.

80 www.irishexaminer.com, 'Ploughing Event – Celebrating Richness of Agriculture', 25 September 2013.

81 Clare Rose of Tralee Centre Blog, April 2013.

82 www.southernstar.ie, 'New Ploughing Book to be Launched in Lisavaird', 18 February 2014.

83 www.npa.ie, History of the NPA & Championships, p. 2.

84 *Weekly Irish Times*, 18 February 2014, p. 6.

85 Watson, 'Backins, Hintins, Ins and Outs and Turnouts', p. 32.

CHAPTER 7
Celebrating farming history: heritage events, heritage centres and museums

1 Wikipedia.org/wiki/Ballyjamesduff

2 Ibid.

3 David Lowenthal, *The Past is a Foreign Country* (Cambridge: Cambridge University Press, 1985), pp 263, 348.

4 Iris Murdoch, *Metaphysics as a Guide to Morals* (London: Vintage, 1992), p. 10.

5 C.R. Badcock, *Lévi-Strauss* (London: Hutchinson, 1975), p. 81.

6 The view we take is close to what has been labelled as a 'constructionist' approach. 'There is no uncritical endorsement … of the correspondence theory of knowledge, but constructionists do share [a] … belief in knowable past reality'. The author of this statement does not believe it is far enough removed from old empiricist approaches, but accepts that it is now a mainstream approach to historical research. Alan Munslow, *The New History* (Harlow: Pearson Educational Limited, 2003), pp 15–16.

7 Eric Hobsbawm, *On History* (London: Wedenfeld & Nicolson, 1997), pp viii, 6.

8 Seamus Heaney, 'The Sense of the Past', *History Ireland*, 1:4 (Dublin, 1993), pp 33–7.

9 Marvin Harris, *Culture, Man and Nature: an Introduction to General Anthropology* (New York: Growell, 1971). Claude Lévi-Strauss, *The Savage Mind* (London: Weidenfeld and Nicolson, 1966 [1972]).

10 Harris, *Prejudice and Tolerance in Ulster*, pp 69–72.

11 Mervyn Watson, 'North Antrim Swing Ploughs: Their Construction and Use', *Ulster Folklife*, 29 (1982), pp 13–23.

12 Séamas MacPhilib, 'Profile of a Landlord in Folk Tradition and in Contemporary Accounts', *Ulster Folklife*, 34 (1988), pp 26–40.

13 'Iconic' is used here in its older sense of an object or activity that participates in the reality it represents. A field of oats in the museum represents the importance of oats in the farming economy of 1900, and at the same time is a real crop, cultivated using authentic techniques.

14 Thomas Mellon, *Thomas Mellon and His Times*, 2nd ed. (Camphill: Centre for Emigration Studies, 1885 [1994]), pp 9, 304–5.

15 E. Estyn Evans, *The Irishness of the Irish* (Armagh: Irish Association, 1965), p. 5.

16 Flann O'Brien, *The Poor Mouth* (*An Béal Bocht*, trans. Patrick C. Power) (London: Pan Books, 1941 [1978]), p. 88.

17 Diarmuid Ó Giolláin, *Locating Irish Folklore: Tradition, Modernity, Identity* (Cork: Cork University Press, 2000), p. 142.

18 E. Estyn Evans, 'Recollections of a Border Childhood', *Ulster Folklife*, 57 (2014).

CONCLUSION

1 Patrick Kavanagh 'Kerr's Ass' from *Collected Poems* (London: Martin Brian & O'Keefe, 1964 [1973]), p. 135.

Select bibliography

Agri-Food Strategy Board, *Going for Growth: A Strategic Action Plan in Support of the Northern Ireland Agri-Food Industry* (Belfast, 2013).

Arensberg, Conrad M. and Solon T. Kimball, *Family and Community in Ireland*, 2nd ed. (Cambridge, MA: Harvard University Press, 1940 [1968]).

Arensberg, Conrad M., *The Irish Countryman: An Anthropological Study* (London: MacMillan, 1937).

Badcock, C.R., *Lévi-Strauss* (London: Hutchinson, 1975).

Barry, Joe, 'Farm Mechanisation' in Brian Lalor (ed.), *The Encyclopaedia of Ireland* (Dublin: Gill & Macmillan, 2003).

Beatson, Robert, 'On Cottages', *The Irish Agricultural Magazine* (Dublin, 1793).

Beattie, Seán, 'The Hiring Fair System in Donegal' in Jim McLaughlin and Seán Beattie (eds), *Atlas of County Donegal* (Cork: Cork University Press, 2013).

Beckett, Samuel, *Malone Dies* (London: Penguin, 1951 [1971]).

Behan, Brendan, *Borstal Boy* (London: Corgi Books, 1958 (1980)).

Bell, Jonathan, 'Economic Change in the Dunfanaghy Area of North Donegal, 1900–1940' (PhD, Queen's University Belfast, 1982).

—— 'Last Sheaves, Ancient Cattle and Protestant Bibles', *Bealóideas* (1985).

—— *Ulster Farming Families, 1930–1960* (Belfast: Ulster Historical Foundation, 2005).

—— and Mervyn Watson, *A History of Irish Farming* (Dublin: Four Courts Press, 2008).

—— and Mervyn Watson, *Farming in North and East County Down: An Oral History* (Downpatrick: Down County Museum, 2011).

—— and Mervyn Watson, *Rooted in the Soil: A History of Cottage Gardens and Allotments in Ireland since 1750* (Dublin: Four Courts Press, 2012).

Berger, John, *Pig Earth* (London: Writers and Readers Publishing Co-operative, 1979).

Bolger, Patrick, *The Irish Co-operative Movement* (Dublin: IAOS, 1977).

Bourke, Joanna, *Husbandry to Housewifery: Women, Economic Change, and Housework in Ireland, 1890–1914* (Oxford: Clarendon Press, 1993).

Boyle, J.W., 'A Marginal Figure: the Irish Rural Labourer' in S. Clarke and J.S. Donnelly (eds), *Irish Peasants: Violence and Unrest* (Madison: University of Wisconsin, 1983).

Carberry, Mary, *The Farm by Lough Gur* (Cork: Mercier Press, 1937 [1973]).

Clifford, John, 'Larne Hiring Fair' in *Poems of John Clifford* (Larne: Larne and District Folklore Society, 1984).

Cohen, A.P., *The Symbolic Construction of Community* (Ellis Horwood Ltd, Chichester and Tavistock Publications, London 1985).

Connolly, S.J., 'Marriage' in Connolly (ed.), *The Oxford Companion to Irish History* (Oxford: Oxford University Press, 1998).

—— 'Cottier' in Connolly (ed.), *The Oxford Companion to Irish History*.

—— 'Seasonal Migration' in Connolly (ed.), *The Oxford Companion to Irish History*.

Corkery, Daniel, *The Hidden Ireland* (Dublin: Gill & Macmillan, 1924 [1973]).

Coyle, Eugene, 'Larkinism and the 1913 County Dublin Farm Labourers' Dispute, 1913', *Dublin Historical Record*, 58:2 (Autumn, 2005).

Crisp, Quentin, *The Naked Civil Servant* (London: Flamingo [1968], 1985).

Curtis, L.P., *Apes and Angel: the Irishman in Victorian Caricature* (London: Smithsonian Institute, 1997).

Daly, Mary E., *The First Department: A History of the Department of Agriculture* (Institute of Public Administration; Dublin, 2002).

Danaher, Kevin, *In Ireland Long Ago* (Cork: Mercier Press, 1962 [1969]).

Department of Agriculture and Technical Instruction for Ireland, *Journal* (Dublin: HMSO, 1918).

Department of Agriculture Ireland, *Annual Report 1942*.

Digby, M., *The World Co-operative Movement* (London: Hutchinson, 1948).

Donald, Eric, 'Agribusiness' in Brian Lalor (ed.), *The Encyclopaedia of Ireland* (Dublin: Gill & Macmillan, 2003).

Donnelly, James S., 'Pastorini and Captain Rock: Millenarianism and Sectarianism in the Rockite Movement 1821–1824' in S. Clark and James S. Donnelly (eds), *Irish Peasants: Violence and Unrest* (Madison: University of Wisconsin, 1983).

Downey, Liam, 'The Cork Butter Exchange', *Ulster Folklife*, 47 (Holywood: Ulster Folk and Transport Museum, 2014).

Evans, Bryce, 'Notorious Anarchists? The Irish smallholder and the state during the Emergency, 1939–45' in William Sheehan and Maura Cronin (eds), *Riotous Assemblies: Rebels, Riots & Revolts* (Cork: Mercier Press, 2011).

Evans, E. Estyn, *The Irishness of the Irish* (Armagh: Irish Association, 1965).

—— *The Personality of Ireland* (Cambridge: Cambridge University Press, 1973 [1992]).

—— 'Recollections of a Border Childhood', *Ulster Folklife*, 57 (2014).

Fitzpatrick, David, 'The Disappearance of the Irish Agricultural Labourer', *Irish Economic and Social History*, 7 (Dublin, 1980).

—— 'A Peculiar Tramping People' in W.E. Vaughan, *A New History of Ireland*, v (Oxford: Clarendon Press, 1989).

Forbes, John, *Memorandums made in Ireland in the Autumn of 1852*, vol. 2 (London: Smith, Elder and Co., 1853).

Gallagher, Sophie, 'Women Rule the Plough … Even in 1957' Boyletm.com/tm/sophie-gallagher.

Gibbon, Peter, 'Arensberg and Kimball Reevisited', *Economy and Society*, 2:4 (1973).

Handley, J.E., *The Irish in Modern Scotland* (Cork: Cork University Press, 1947).

Hannan, Damian, *Rural Exodus* (London: Chapman, 1970).

—— *Displacement and Development: Class, Kinship and Social Change in Irish Rural Communities* (Dublin: Economic and Social Research Institute, 1979).

Hannan, Robbie and Jonathan Bell, 'The Bothóg' in Trefor M. Owen (ed.), *From Corrib to Cultra* (Holywood: Ulster Folk and Transport Museum, 2000).

Harris, Marvin, *Culture, Man and Nature: An Introduction to General Anthropology* (New York: Growell, 1971).

Harris, Rosemary, *Prejudice and Tolerance in Ulster* (Manchester: Manchester University Press, 1972).

Harris, Ruth-Ann, 'Migratory Labour' in Brian Lalor (ed.), *The Encyclopaedia of Ireland* (Dublin: Gill & Macmillan, 2003).

Heaney, Seamus, 'The Sense of the Past', *History Ireland*, 1:4 (Dublin, 1993).

Henry, Paul, *An Irish Portrait: the Autobiography of Paul Henry* (London: Batsford, 1952).

Hewitt, John, *The Day of the Corncrake: Poems of the Nine Glens* (Belfast: Glens of Antrim Historical Society, 1969).

Hobsbawm, Eric, *On History* (London: Wedenfeld & Nicolson, 1997).

Holmes, Heather, *Tattie Howkers: Irish Potato Workers in Ayrshire* (Ayr: Ayrshire Archaeological and Natural History Society, 2005).

Irish Farmers' Journal and Weekly Intelligencer

Irish Farmers' Association, *People and the Land* (Dublin: IFA, 1972).

Kavanagh, Gaynor, *Dream Spaces: Memory and the Museum* (London: University of Leicester Press, 2000).

Kavanagh, Patrick, *Collected Poems* (London: Martin Brian and O'Keefe, 1972 [1973]).

Kelleher, Carmel and Ann O'Mahony, *Marginalisation in Irish Agriculture* (Dublin: An Foras Talúntas, 1984).

Kinmouth, Claudia, *Irish Rural Interiors* (New Haven: Yale, 2006).

Lévi-Strauss, Claude, *The Savage Mind* (London: Weidenfeld and Nicolson, 1966 [1972]).

Lowenthal, David, *The Past is a Foreign Country* (Cambridge: Cambridge University Press, 1985).

MacDonagh, Oliver, 'The Economy and Society 1830–45' in W.E. Vaughan (ed.), *A New History of Ireland*, v (Oxford: Clarendon Press, 1989).

McGahern, John, *The Dark* (London: Faber & Faber, 1965).

MacGill, Patrick, *Children of the Dead End* (Ascot: Caliban Books, 1914 [1970]).

MacPhilib, Séamas, 'Profile of a Landlord in Folk Tradition and in Contemporary Accounts', *Ulster Folklife*, 34 (1988).

Marx, Karl, 'The Eighteenth Brumaire of Louis Bonaparte' in Karl Marx and Frederick Engels, *Selected Works* (London: Lawrence and Wishart (1968 [1980]).

—— and Friedrich Engels, *The Communist Manifesto* (Fairford: Echo Library, 1848 [2009]).

Mason, W.S., *An Account of Ireland, Statistical and Political* (London, 1814).

Mellon, Thomas, *Thomas Mellon and His Times*, 2nd ed. (Camphill: Centre for Emigration Studies, 1885 [1994].

Messenger, John E., '*Man of Aran* Revisited' *University Review*, 3:9 (Dublin, 1963).

—— lecture, Queens University of Belfast, 1968.

—— *Inis Beag, Isle of Ireland* (New York: Holt, Rinehart and Winston, 1969).

Micks, W.L. *An Account of the … Congested Districts Board for Ireland, from 1891 to 1923* (Dublin: Eason & Sons, 1925).

Ministry of Agriculture for Northern Ireland, *The Conditions of Employment of Agricultural Workers in Northern Ireland* (Belfast: HMSO, 1938).

Murdoch, Iris, *The Red and the Green* (New York: Avon Books, 1965).

—— *Metaphysics as a Guide to Morals* (London: Vintage, 1992).

Nicholson, Asenath, *Ireland's Welcome to the Stranger* (Dublin: Lilliput Press, 2002).

O'Brien, Edna, *The Country Girls* (London: Penguin [1960], 1987).

O'Brien, Flann, *The Poor Mouth* (*An Béal Bocht*, trans. Patrick C. Power) (London: Pan Books, 1941 [1978]).

O'Donnell, Peadar, 'The Irish Labour Movement: the Scottish Dimension'. Lecture given at a conference organised by the Irish Labour History Society in 1981.

O'Dowd, Anne, *Meitheal: A Study of Co-operative Labour in Rural Ireland* (Comhairle Bhéaloideas Éireann: Dublin, 1981).

—— *Spalpeens and Tattie Hokers* (Dublin: Irish Academic Press, 1991).

Ó Faolain, Seán, 'Magical Ireland' in *Countrygoer: Introducing Ireland* (London, 1947).

Ó Giolláin, Diarmuid, 'Perspectives in the Study of Folk-Religion', *Ulster Folklife*, 36 (1990).

—— *Locating Irish Folklore: Tradition, Modernity, Identity* (Cork: Cork University Press, 2000).

Ó Gráda, Cormac, 'Poverty, Population and Agriculture, 1801–45' in W.E. Vaughan (ed.), *A New History of Ireland*, v (Oxford: Clarendon Press, 1989).

O'Neill, Kevin, *Family and Farm in Pre-Famine Ireland* (Madison, WI: University Press, 1984).

Popkin, S.L., 'The Rational Peasant', *Theory and Society*, 9:3 (1980).

Sacks, Paul M., *The Donegal Mafia: An Irish Political Machine* (New Haven: Yale University Press, 1976).

Sage, Lorna, *Bad Blood* (London: Fourth Estate, 2001).

Sayers, Peig, *Peig* (Dublin: Comhlacht Oideachais n hÉireann, 1936 (1969)).

—— *The Autobiography of Peig Sayers* (trans. Bryan MacMahon) (Syracuse NY: Syracuse University Press, 1974).

Siamsa Tíre, *Publicity brochure* (Finuge, 1971).

Sinn Féin, *Eire Nua: The Social and Economic Programme of Sinn Féin* (Dublin: Sinn Féin, 1971).

Stewart, A.T.Q., *The Shape of Irish History* (Belfast: McGill-Queen's University Press, 2001).

Synge, John Millington, *The Playboy of the Western World* (Oxford: Oxford University Press, 1998).

Thompson, E.P., *The Making of the English Working Class* (London: Penguin, 1963 [1980]).

Trevor, William, 'The Ballroom of Romance' in *The Ballroom of Romance and Other Stories* (London: The Bodley Head, 1972).

Turner, Victor, *The Forest of Symbols* (Ithaca, NY; Cornell University Press, 1967).

—— *A Celebration of Ritual* (Washington DC: Smithsonian Institution, 1982).

Tynan, Katherine, *Peeps at Many Lands: Ireland* (London: Black, 1909).

Ua Duinnín, An tAthair Padraig, *Amhráin Eoghan Ruaidh Uí Súilleabháin* (Gaelic League: Dublin, 1901).

Wallace, M.G., 'The Earnings of Irish Migratory Labourers in England and Scotland, Season 1904', Department of Agriculture and Technical Instruction for Ireland, *Journal* (Dublin, 1905).

Watson, Mervyn, 'North Antrim Swing Ploughs: Their Construction and Use', *Ulster Folklife*, 29 (Holywood, 1982).

—— 'Standardisation of Pig Production: the Case of the Large White Ulster Pig', *Ulster Folklife*, 34 (1988).

—— 'Backins, hintins, ins and outs and turnouts: a study of horse ploughing societies in Northern Ireland' (MA, Queen's University Belfast, 1991).

—— 'Irish Moiled Cattle', *Ulster Folklife*, 36 (1990).

—— 'The Role of the Horse on Irish Farms' in Trefor M. Owen (ed.), *From Corrib to Cultra* (Institute of Irish Studies, Queen's University Belfast in association with the Ulster Folk and Transport Museum, 2000).

Wilson, Thomas M., and Hastings Donnan, *The Anthropology of Ireland* (Oxford, Berg, 2006).

Young, Arthur, *A Tour in Ireland*, 2 vols (London, 1780).

Index